About This Book

2014 primary curriculum

The 2014 UK primary curriculum has statutory requirements for which spelling patterns and words should be taught in each year group.

This book meets these requirements by covering the new spelling patterns and words that are specified for Year 5 and Year 6 in the 2014 curriculum.

Our Year 5 books revise the spelling work covered in previous years before Year 5.

Versions of the book

There are 3 versions available:
- plain text (with no words to trace over)
- cursive / joined up **WITHOUT** lead-in strokes
- cursive / joined up **WITH** lead-in strokes (not available on Amazon, only available to download from SaveTeachersSundays.com)

Accompanying resources

- passwords for over 350 Spelling games included in the book
- lesson plans, dictation sentences and other teaching resources available to purchase separately on SaveTeachersSundays.com

Contents

Contents

The sound (shus) is often represented by the letters cious when it comes at the end of words, like in the words below.

Remember: Say the word aloud, then say each letter aloud **as you write it** e.g. 'conscious, c ... o ... n ... s ... c ... i ... o ... u ... s'

If you are **conscious (con/scious)** of something, you think about it.
_____ _____ _____ _____
_____ _____ _____ _____

If something is **precious (pre/cious)** to you, you care about it a lot.
_____ _____ _____ _____
_____ _____ _____ _____

A criminal needs to try not to look **suspicious (su/spi/cious)**.
_____ _____ _____ _____
_____ _____ _____ _____

Delicious (de/li/cious) means very tasty.
_____ _____ _____ _____

An alligator is a **vicious (vi/cious)** animal.
_____ _____ _____ _____
_____ _____ _____ _____

A **spacious (spa/cious)** room is one that has lots of space in it.
_____ _____ _____ _____
_____ _____ _____ _____

To be **gracious (gra/cious)** means to be kind and polite.
_____ _____ _____ _____
_____ _____ _____ _____

Ferocious (fe/ro/cious) means very fierce.
_____ _____ _____ _____
_____ _____ _____ _____

To be **malicious (ma/li/cious)** means to be cruel and nasty.
_____ _____ _____ _____
_____ _____ _____ _____

If you are **tenacious (te/na/cious)** then you never give up.
_____ _____ _____ _____
_____ _____ _____ _____

Now test yourself without looking at the words and **check for yourself** if you got them all right. Practice writing any words that you made mistakes on again.

The sound (shus) is often represented by the letters tious when it comes at the end of words. The word anxious is one of very few words that end in xious.

Remember: Say the word aloud, then say each letter aloud **as you write it** e.g. 'ambitious, a ... m ... b ... i ... t ... i ... o ... u ... s'

If you are **ambitious (am/bi/tious)**, you want to achieve a lot.
_____   _____   _____   _____
_____   _____   _____   _____

To be **cautious (cau/tious)** means to be careful.
_____   _____   _____   _____
_____   _____   _____   _____

If a disease is **infectious (in/fec/tious)** it will spread between people.
_____   _____   _____   _____
_____   _____   _____   _____

If food is **nutritious (nu/tri/tious)** then it is good for you.
_____   _____   _____   _____
_____   _____   _____   _____

To be **pretentious (pre/ten/tious)** means to think that you are important.
_____   _____   _____   _____
_____   _____   _____   _____

Fictitious (fic/ti/tious) means made-up or not real.   _____
_____   _____   _____   _____
_____   _____   _____   _____

To be **superstitious (su/per/sti/tious)** means to believe in luck and omens.
_____   _____   _____   _____
_____   _____   _____   _____

If someone is **fractious (frac/tious)** he or she is argumentative.
_____   _____   _____   _____
_____   _____   _____   _____

If something is **vexatious (vex/a/tious)** it makes people angry.
_____   _____   _____   _____
_____   _____   _____   _____

If you are **anxious (an/xious)** then you are worried and nervous.
_____   _____   _____   _____
_____   _____   _____   _____

Now test yourself without looking at the words and **check for yourself** if you got them all right. Practice writing any words that you made mistakes on again.

The sound (shul) is often represented by the letters cial when it comes at the end of words, like in the words below.

Remember: Say the word aloud, then say each letter aloud **as you write it** e.g. 'social, s ... o ... c ... i ... a ... l'

A **social (so/cial)** event is one where people meet other people.
_____ _____ _____ _____
_____ _____ _____ _____

People's friends are **special (spe/cial)** to them.
_____ _____ _____ _____
_____ _____ _____ _____

A football referee is an **official (of/fi/cial)**.
_____ _____ _____ _____
_____ _____ _____ _____

Banks are part of the **financial (fi/nan/cial)** system.
_____ _____ _____ _____
_____ _____ _____ _____

A **commercial (com/mer/cial)** is an advert on television.
_____ _____ _____ _____
_____ _____ _____ _____

Crucial (cru/cial) means very important.
_____ _____ _____ _____
_____ _____ _____ _____

Plastic flowers are **artificial (ar/ti/fi/cial)**.
_____ _____ _____ _____
_____ _____ _____ _____

If something is **beneficial (ben/e/fi/cial)** for you, it is good for you.
_____ _____ _____ _____
_____ _____ _____ _____

If something is **superficial (su/per/fi/cial)** it is not really important.
_____ _____ _____ _____
_____ _____ _____ _____

Beards and moustaches are **facial (fa/cial)** hair.
_____ _____ _____ _____
_____ _____ _____ _____

Now test yourself without looking at the words and **<u>check for yourself</u>** if you got them all right. Practice writing any words that you made mistakes on again.

The sound (shul) is often represented by the letters tial when it comes at the end of words, like in the words below.

Remember: Say the word aloud, then say each letter aloud **as you write it** e.g. 'partial, p ... a ... r ... t ... i ... a ... l'

If you are **partial (par/tial)** to cake, that means that you like cake.
_____   _____   _____   _____
_____   _____   _____   _____

If you have **potential (po/ten/tial)**, you might do very well in the future.
_____   _____   _____   _____
_____   _____   _____   _____

If something is **essential (es/sen/tial)** then it is very important.
_____   _____   _____   _____
_____   _____   _____   _____

Initial (in/i/tial) means first.
_____   _____   _____   _____
_____   _____   _____   _____

A **substantial (sub/stan/tial)** amount of money is a large amount of money.
_____   _____   _____   _____
_____   _____   _____   _____

If information is **confidential (con/fi/den/tial)** then it is kept secret.
_____   _____   _____   _____
_____   _____   _____   _____

A football referee needs to be **impartial (im/par/tial)**.
_____   _____   _____   _____
_____   _____   _____   _____

Torrential (tor/ren/tial) rain is very heavy rain.
_____   _____   _____   _____
_____   _____   _____   _____

Palatial (pa/la/tial) means luxurious.
_____   _____   _____   _____
_____   _____   _____   _____

Karate and judo are **martial (mar/tial)** arts.
_____   _____   _____   _____
_____   _____   _____   _____

Now test yourself without looking at the words and **check for yourself** if you got them all right. Practice writing any words that you made mistakes on again.

© www.SaveTeachersSundays.com 2013

The sound (unt) is often represented by the letters ant when it comes at the end of words, like in the words below.

Remember: Say the word aloud, then say each letter aloud **as you write it** e.g. 'brilliant, b ... r ... i ... l ... l ... i ... a ... n ... t'

Brilliant (bril/li/ant) means very good.
_____ _____ _____ _____
_____ _____ _____ _____

If something is **significant (sig/ni/fi/cant)**, that means it is important.
_____ _____ _____ _____
_____ _____ _____ _____

Numbers are **relevant (rel/e/vant)** to maths.
_____ _____ _____ _____
_____ _____ _____ _____

A **servant (ser/vant)** serves a master.
_____ _____ _____ _____
_____ _____ _____ _____

An **assistant (as/sis/tant)** helps someone more senior than him or her.
_____ _____ _____ _____
_____ _____ _____ _____

A **constant (con/stant)** noise is a noise that does not stop.
_____ _____ _____ _____
_____ _____ _____ _____

Pleasant (plea/sant) is another word for nice.
_____ _____ _____ _____
_____ _____ _____ _____

If you are **hesitant (he/si/tant)**, then you are not sure what to do.
_____ _____ _____ _____
_____ _____ _____ _____

An **infant (in/fant)** is a young child.
_____ _____ _____ _____
_____ _____ _____ _____

If you are **observant (ob/ser/vant)** then you notice things.
_____ _____ _____ _____
_____ _____ _____ _____

Now test yourself without looking at the words and **check for yourself** if you got them all right. Practice writing any words that you made mistakes on again.

The sound (unt) is most often represented by the letters ent when it comes at the end of words, like in the words below.

Remember: Say the word aloud, then say each letter aloud **as you write it** e.g. 'moment, m ... o ... m ... e ... n ... t'

A **moment (mo/ment)** is a very small amount of time.

_____ _____ _____ _____
_____ _____ _____ _____

A **present (pre/sent)** is another word for a gift.

_____ _____ _____ _____
_____ _____ _____ _____

If you are **patient (pa/tient)**, you are prepared to wait.

_____ _____ _____ _____
_____ _____ _____ _____

A **student (stu/dent)** is someone who goes to school, college or university.

_____ _____ _____ _____
_____ _____ _____ _____

If you are **independent (in/de/pen/dent)**, then you do things for yourself.

_____ _____ _____ _____
_____ _____ _____ _____

A **client (cli/ent)** pays someone to do a job.

_____ _____ _____ _____
_____ _____ _____ _____

If you **document (doc/u/ment)** an event, you write about it.

_____ _____ _____ _____
_____ _____ _____ _____

A **current (cur/rent)** moves the water in a river below its surface.

_____ _____ _____ _____
_____ _____ _____ _____

An **incident (in/ci/dent)** is another name for an event.

_____ _____ _____ _____
_____ _____ _____ _____

An estate **agent (a/gent)** is someone who sells houses.

_____ _____ _____ _____
_____ _____ _____ _____

Now test yourself without looking at the words and **check for yourself** if you got them all right. Practice writing any words that you made mistakes on again.

The sound (unt) is most often represented by the letters ent when it comes at the end of words, like in the words below.

Remember: Say the word aloud, then say each letter aloud **as you write it** e.g. 'talent, t ... a ... l ... e ... n ... t'

If you have a **talent (ta/lent)** for something then you are good at it.
_____ _____ _____ _____
_____ _____ _____ _____

A science **experiment (ex/pe/ri/ment)** tests an idea.
_____ _____ _____ _____

Excellent (ex/cel/lent) means very good.
_____ _____ _____ _____

Equivalent (e/qui/va/lent) means worth the same.
_____ _____ _____ _____

If you have **sufficient (suf/fi/cient)** food, you have enough food.
_____ _____ _____ _____

If something is **apparent (ap/pa/rent)** then it is obvious.
_____ _____ _____ _____

Ancient (an/cient) means very old.
_____ _____ _____ _____

In sport an **opponent (op/po/nent)** is someone that you try to beat.
_____ _____ _____ _____

If something is **permanent (per/ma/nent)** then it lasts for a long time.
_____ _____ _____ _____

If something is **ur (ur/gent)** then it needs to done quickly.
_____ _____ _____ _____

Now test yourself without looking at the words and **check for yourself** if you got them all right. Practice writing any words that you made mistakes on again.

The sound (unt) is most often represented by the letters ent when it comes at the end of words, like in the words below.

Remember: Say the word aloud, then say each letter aloud **as you write it** e.g. 'silent, s ... i ... l ... e ... n ... t'

If it is **silent (si/lent)** then there is no noise at all.
_____ _____ _____ _____
_____ _____ _____ _____

To be **efficient (ef/fi/cient)** means to be quick and effective.
_____ _____ _____ _____
_____ _____ _____ _____

In a **tournament (tour/na/ment)** people or teams play against each other.
_____ _____ _____ _____
_____ _____ _____ _____

You speak with the same **accent (ac/cent)** as other people from your area.
_____ _____ _____ _____
_____ _____ _____ _____

If you are **confident (con/fi/dent)** then you believe in yourself.
_____ _____ _____ _____
_____ _____ _____ _____

To be **consistent (con/sis/tent)** means that you are the same all the time.
_____ _____ _____ _____
_____ _____ _____ _____

Frequent (fre/quent) means often.
_____ _____ _____ _____
_____ _____ _____ _____

If someone is **violent (vi/o/lent)** then they hurt other people.
_____ _____ _____ _____
_____ _____ _____ _____

To be **innocent (in/no/cent)** means to have not done anything wrong.
_____ _____ _____ _____
_____ _____ _____ _____

To be a **decent (de/cent)** person means to be kind.
_____ _____ _____ _____
_____ _____ _____ _____

Now test yourself without looking at the words and **check for yourself** if you got them all right. Practice writing any words that you made mistakes on again.

The sound (uns) is often represented by the letters ance when it comes at the end of words, like in the words below.

Remember: Say the word aloud, then say each letter aloud **as you write it** e.g. 'balance, b ... a ... l ... a ... n ... c ... e'

Can you **balance (ba/lance)** yourself on one leg?
_____ _____ _____ _____
_____ _____ _____ _____

A theatre puts on a **performance (per/for/mance)** every day.
_____ _____ _____ _____
_____ _____ _____ _____

Your health is of more **importance (im/por/tance)** than anything else.
_____ _____ _____ _____
_____ _____ _____ _____

One lap of an athletics track is a **distance (dis/tance)** of 400m.
_____ _____ _____ _____
_____ _____ _____ _____

Clowns try to have a funny **appearance (ap/pear/ance)**.
_____ _____ _____ _____
_____ _____ _____ _____

You come into a place through the **entrance (en/trance)** to it.
_____ _____ _____ _____
_____ _____ _____ _____

If you show **reluctance (re/luc/tance)** you do not want to do something.
_____ _____ _____ _____
_____ _____ _____ _____

If you dance with **elegance (el/e/gance)**, you dance with style and grace.
_____ _____ _____ _____
_____ _____ _____ _____

An **ambulance (am/bu/lance)** takes injured people to hospital.
_____ _____ _____ _____
_____ _____ _____ _____

Someone who is a **nuisance (nui/sance)** annoys other people.
_____ _____ _____ _____
_____ _____ _____ _____

Now test yourself without looking at the words and **check for yourself** if you got them all right. Practice writing any words that you made mistakes on again.

© www.SaveTeachersSundays.com 2013

The sound (uns) is often represented by the letters ence when it comes at the end of words, like in the words below.

Remember: Say the word aloud, then say each letter aloud **as you write it** e.g. 'science, s ... c ... i ... e ... n ... c ... e'

In **science (sci/ence)** you learn about biology, physics and chemistry.
_____ _____ _____ _____
_____ _____ _____ _____

An **experience (ex/per/i/ence)** is something that you do, like a sky dive.
_____ _____ _____ _____

Police collect **evidence (ev/i/dence)** against criminals, like finger prints.
_____ _____ _____ _____
_____ _____ _____ _____

The **difference (dif/fer/ence)** between ten and forty is thirty.
_____ _____ _____ _____

To **influence (in/flu/ence)** people means to persuade them.
_____ _____ _____ _____

If you have **presence (pre/sence)**, people are impressed when meeting you.
_____ _____ _____ _____

A **sentence (sen/tence)** describes how long someone will be in prison for.
_____ _____ _____ _____
_____ _____ _____ _____

At an event, the **audience (au/di/ence)** are the people watching the event.
_____ _____ _____ _____

An **absence (ab/sence)** from school means not going to school.
_____ _____ _____ _____

2, 4, 6, 8, 10 is a **sequence (se/quence)** of numbers.
_____ _____ _____ _____

Now test yourself without looking at the words and **check for yourself** if you got them all right. Practice writing any words that you made mistakes on again.

Some of the words below end in ancy, like infancy; some of the words end in ency, like agency.

Remember: Say the word aloud, then say each letter aloud **as you write it** e.g. 'infancy, i … n … f … a … n … c … y'

In its **infancy (in/fan/cy)**, an animal relies on its parent/s.
_____ _____ _____ _____
_____ _____ _____ _____

Before a sky dive, most people feel **hesitancy (he/si/tan/cy)**.
_____ _____ _____ _____

An estate **agency (a/gen/cy)** sells houses.
_____ _____ _____ _____
_____ _____ _____ _____

In an **emergency (e/mer/gen/cy)** you should dial 999.
_____ _____ _____ _____

The British **currency (cur/ren/cy)** is pounds sterling.
_____ _____ _____ _____
_____ _____ _____ _____

Newer car engines have better **efficiency (e/fi/cien/cy)** than older ones.
_____ _____ _____ _____

Each radio station has its own **frequency (fre/quen/cy)**, like 104.9 XFM.
_____ _____ _____ _____
_____ _____ _____ _____

The weather has a **tendency (ten/den/cy)** to be warmer in summer.
_____ _____ _____ _____

If you do wrong, you should have the **decency (de/cency)** to say sorry.
_____ _____ _____ _____
_____ _____ _____ _____

The **potency (po/ten/cy)** of a medicine means how strong it is.
_____ _____ _____ _____
_____ _____ _____ _____

Now test yourself without looking at the words and **check for yourself** if you got them all right. Practice writing any words that you made mistakes on again.

The letters ough are used to represent several different sounds in the words below.

Remember: Say the word aloud, then say each letter aloud **as you write it** e.g. 'rough, r ... o ... u ... g ... h'

You should try not to be too **rough** when you play with younger children.

_____ _____ _____ _____
_____ _____ _____ _____

If meat is hard to chew, you might say that it is **tough**.

_____ _____ _____ _____
_____ _____ _____ _____

Did you have **enough** to eat in your last meal?

_____ _____ _____ _____
_____ _____ _____ _____

When you are ill, you might have a **cough**.

_____ _____ _____ _____
_____ _____ _____ _____

Even **though** these words are hard, you need to learn to spell them.

_____ _____ _____ _____
_____ _____ _____ _____

Dough is baked to make bread.

_____ _____ _____ _____
_____ _____ _____ _____

You come into a room **through** the door.

_____ _____ _____ _____
_____ _____ _____ _____

If you check your work carefully, you are being **thorough**.

_____ _____ _____ _____
_____ _____ _____ _____

A **borough** is a part of a city, like Westminster is a **borough** of London.

_____ _____ _____ _____
_____ _____ _____ _____

A **plough** is used by a farmer to break up soil.

_____ _____ _____ _____
_____ _____ _____ _____

Now test yourself without looking at the words and <u>check for yourself</u> if you got them all right. Practice writing any words that you made mistakes on again.

© www.SaveTeachersSundays.com 2013

Some of the words below end in ought, like bought; some of the words end in aught, like taught.

Remember: Say the word aloud, then say each letter aloud **as you write it** e.g. 'ought, o ... u ... g ... h ... t'

You **ought** to always try your hardest at school.
_____ _____ _____   _____
_____ _____ _____   _____

What was the last thing that you **bought** in a shop?
_____ _____ _____   _____
_____ _____ _____   _____

A **thought** is an idea that you have in your head.
_____ _____ _____   _____
_____ _____ _____   _____

Nought is another name for zero.
_____ _____ _____   _____
_____ _____ _____   _____

To have **sought** for something means to have searched for it.
_____ _____ _____   _____
_____ _____ _____   _____

Have you **brought** your homework to school today?
_____ _____ _____   _____
_____ _____ _____   _____

After a boxer has **fought** a long fight, he will probably be tired.
_____ _____ _____   _____
_____ _____ _____   _____

Has your teacher **taught** you much this year?
_____ _____ _____   _____
_____ _____ _____   _____

Have you ever **caught** a fish?
_____ _____ _____   _____
_____ _____ _____   _____

Swimming with sharks is **fraught** with danger.
_____ _____ _____   _____
_____ _____ _____   _____

Now test yourself without looking at the words and **check for yourself** if you got them all right. Practice writing any words that you made mistakes on again.

When the syllable containing the letters fer is stressed (emphasised), the r is doubled. However when this syllable is not stressed, the r is not doubled.

Remember: Say the word aloud, then say each letter aloud **as you write it** e.g. 'referred, r ... e ... f ... e ... r ... r ... e ... d'

You are **referred (re/fer/red)** to by your name.
_____ _____ _____ _____
_____ _____ _____ _____

Who are you **referring (re/fer/ring)** to?
_____ _____ _____ _____
_____ _____ _____ _____

The children's stories **differed (dif/fered)** about who did what.
_____ _____ _____ _____
_____ _____ _____ _____

Some people are always **differing (dif/fer/ing)** with everyone else.
_____ _____ _____ _____
_____ _____ _____ _____

A religious **offering (of/fer/ing)** is meant as a gift for God.
_____ _____ _____ _____
_____ _____ _____ _____

If you are in pain, then you are **suffering (suf/fer/ing)**.
_____ _____ _____ _____
_____ _____ _____ _____

"Which game are you **preferring (pre/fer/ring)**?" asked Dad.
_____ _____ _____ _____
_____ _____ _____ _____

Do you have a **preference (pre/fer/ence)** for water over milk?
_____ _____ _____ _____
_____ _____ _____ _____

When you leave a job, your boss writes you a **reference (re/fer/ence)**.
_____ _____ _____ _____
_____ _____ _____ _____

A **referee (re/fer/ee)** is in charge of a football match.
_____ _____ _____ _____
_____ _____ _____ _____

Now test yourself without looking at the words and **check for yourself** if you got them all right. Practice writing any words that you made mistakes on again.

A number of base words end in the letters able, like in the words below.

Remember: Say the word aloud, then say each letter aloud **as you write it** e.g. 'capable, c ... a ... p ... a ... b ... l ... e'

If you are **capable (ca/pa/ble)** of something, that means you can do it.

_____   _____   _____   _____

_____   _____   _____   _____

An event is sold out if it has no more tickets **available (a/vai/la/ble)**.

_____   _____   _____   _____

_____   _____   _____   _____

The acronym PC can stand for police **constable (con/sta/ble)**.

_____   _____   _____   _____

_____   _____   _____   _____

A potato is a type of **vegetable (ve/ge/ta/ble)**.

_____   _____   _____   _____

_____   _____   _____   _____

If something is **inevitable (i/ne/vi/ta/ble)**, there is no way to stop it.

_____   _____   _____   _____

_____   _____   _____   _____

If someone is **vulnerable (vul/ne/ra/ble)**, he or she is easily hurt or upset.

_____   _____   _____   _____

_____   _____   _____   _____

A **syllable (syl/la/ble)** is a beat in a word.

_____   _____   _____   _____

_____   _____   _____   _____

Probable (pro/ba/ble) is another word for likely.

_____   _____   _____   _____

_____   _____   _____   _____

If an opponent is **formidable (for/mi/da/ble)**, then they are hard to beat.

_____   _____   _____   _____

_____   _____   _____   _____

A **parable (pa/ra/ble)** is a religious story that tries to teach a lesson.

_____   _____   _____   _____

_____   _____   _____   _____

Now test yourself without looking at the words and **check for yourself** if you got them all right. Practice writing any words that you made mistakes on again.

Each of the words below has a base word (that makes sense on its own), with the suffix able added to the end of it.

Remember: Say the word aloud, then say each letter aloud **as you write it** e.g. 'reasonable, r ... e ... a ... s ... o ... n ... a ... b ... l ... e'

To be **reasonable (reason+able)** means to be fair.
_____ _____ _____
_____ _____ _____

If something is **suitable (suit+able)** that means that it is OK.
_____ _____ _____
_____ _____ _____

A **considerable (consider+able)** amount means a large amount.
_____ _____ _____
_____ _____ _____

A sofa needs to be **comfortable (comfort+able)** to sit on.
_____ _____ _____
_____ _____ _____

If something is **acceptable (accept+able)**, it is good enough.
_____ _____ _____
_____ _____ _____

Remarkable (remark+able) is another word for surprising or unusual.
_____ _____ _____
_____ _____ _____

If something is **fashionable (fashion+able)**, it is popular at the moment.
_____ _____ _____
_____ _____ _____

Miserable (miser+able) means very sad.
_____ _____ _____
_____ _____ _____

If a film is **predictable (predict+able)**, you can guess what will happen.
_____ _____ _____
_____ _____ _____

A **portable (port+able)** MP3 player is one that you can take anywhere.
_____ _____ _____
_____ _____ _____

Now test yourself without looking at the words and **check for yourself** if you got them all right. Practice writing any words that you made mistakes on again.

Sometimes when suffix able is added to base words ending in e, the e is dropped. When the suffix able is added to a base word ending in y, the y is changed to i.

Remember: Say the word aloud, then say each letter aloud **as you write it** e.g. 'valuable, v ... a ... l ... u ... a ... b ... l ... e'

If something is **valuable (value+able)**, it is worth a lot of money.
_____ _____ _____ _____
_____ _____ _____ _____

If something is **desirable (desire+able)** that means people want it.
_____ _____ _____ _____
_____ _____ _____ _____

If something is **notable (note+able)**, it is out of the ordinary.
_____ _____ _____ _____
_____ _____ _____ _____

If something is **admirable (admire+able)**, people admire it.
_____ _____ _____ _____
_____ _____ _____ _____

If something is **advisable (advise+able)**, it is a good idea.
_____ _____ _____ _____
_____ _____ _____ _____

If something is **variable (vary+able)**, it changes.
_____ _____ _____ _____
_____ _____ _____ _____

If something is **reliable (rely+able)**, it does not break or fail.
_____ _____ _____ _____
_____ _____ _____ _____

People are **identifiable (identify+able)** because we all look different.
_____ _____ _____ _____
_____ _____ _____ _____

If there is a good reason for doing something, it is **justifiable (justify+able)**.
_____ _____ _____ _____
_____ _____ _____ _____

If something is definitely true, then it is **undeniable (undeny+able)**.
_____ _____ _____ _____
_____ _____ _____ _____

Now test yourself without looking at the words and **check for yourself** if you got them all right. Practice writing any words that you made mistakes on again.

Name: _____   Date: _____   **Suffix able 3**

Sometimes when suffix able is added to base words ending in e, the e is dropped.
However, sometimes the e is kept, like in the words below.

Remember: Say the word aloud, then say each letter aloud **as you write it** e.g.
'sizeable, s ... i ... z ... e ... a ... b ... l ... e'

If something is **sizeable (size+able)**, it is big.
_____ _____ _____ _____
_____ _____ _____ _____

If the weather is **changeable (change+able)** it can be nice, then not nice.
_____ _____ _____ _____
_____ _____ _____ _____

If something is **noticeable (notice+able)**, it stands out.
_____ _____ _____ _____
_____ _____ _____ _____

If something is **manageable (manage+able)**, it is doable.
_____ _____ _____ _____
_____ _____ _____ _____

If something is **irreplaceable (irreplace+able)**, it cannot be replaced.
_____ _____ _____ _____
_____ _____ _____ _____

A lot of people think that puppies are **loveable (love+able)**.
_____ _____ _____ _____
_____ _____ _____ _____

If someone is **likeable (like+able)**, people normally like him or her.
_____ _____ _____ _____
_____ _____ _____ _____

If someone is **knowledgeable (knowledge+able)**, he or she knows a lot.
_____ _____ _____ _____
_____ _____ _____ _____

Rules and laws need to be **enforceable (enforce+able)**.
_____ _____ _____ _____
_____ _____ _____ _____

A **rechargeable (recharge+able)** battery can be used more than once.
_____ _____ _____ _____
_____ _____ _____ _____

Now test yourself without looking at the words and **check for yourself** if you got
them all right. Practice writing any words that you made mistakes on again.

© www.SaveTeachersSundays.com 2013

18

A number of base words end in the letters ible, like in the words below.

Remember: Say the word aloud, then say each letter aloud **as you write it** e.g. 'possible, p ... o ... s ... s ... i ... b ... l ... e'

If something is **possible (pos/si/ble)**, that means that it can be done.
_____ _____ _____ _____
_____ _____ _____ _____

You are **responsible (re/spon/si/ble)** for your actions.
_____ _____ _____ _____
_____ _____ _____ _____

Terrible (ter/ri/ble) means very bad.
_____ _____ _____ _____
_____ _____ _____ _____

If something is **visible (vi/si/ble)**, that means that it can be seen.
_____ _____ _____ _____
_____ _____ _____ _____

You need to behave in a **sensible (sen/si/ble)** way.
_____ _____ _____ _____
_____ _____ _____ _____

If a material is **flexible (flex/i/ble)**, it can be bent without breaking.
_____ _____ _____ _____
_____ _____ _____ _____

Bullying other children is a **horrible (hor/ri/ble)** thing to do.
_____ _____ _____ _____
_____ _____ _____ _____

Incredible (in/cre/di/ble) is another word for amazing.
_____ _____ _____ _____
_____ _____ _____ _____

If food is **irresistible (ir/re/sis/ti/ble)**, it is hard to say no to.
_____ _____ _____ _____
_____ _____ _____ _____

Plausible (plau/si/ble) is another word for believable.
_____ _____ _____ _____
_____ _____ _____ _____

Now test yourself without looking at the words and **check for yourself** if you got them all right. Practice writing any words that you made mistakes on again.

Some words have silent letters in them. All of the words below contain the letters mb, but the letter b is silent.

Remember: Say the word aloud, then say each letter aloud **as you write it** e.g. 'lamb, l ... a ... m ... b'

A **lamb** is a baby sheep.

_____   _____   _____   _____

_____   _____   _____   _____

A **plumber** fixes blocked and broken drains and pipes.

_____   _____   _____   _____

A **comb** is used to straighten hair.

_____   _____   _____   _____

_____   _____   _____   _____

A **bomb** explodes.

_____   _____   _____   _____

Your arm is a **limb**.

_____   _____   _____   _____

_____   _____   _____   _____

If a part of your body is **numb** that means that you cannot feel it.

_____   _____   _____   _____

A **crumb** is a tiny piece of bread, cake or biscuit.

_____   _____   _____   _____

_____   _____   _____   _____

You have one **thumb** on each hand.

_____   _____   _____   _____

A **tomb** is a place for burying a dead person.

_____   _____   _____   _____

_____   _____   _____   _____

Would you like to **climb** a mountain?

_____   _____   _____   _____

_____   _____   _____   _____

Now test yourself without looking at the words and **check for yourself** if you got them all right. Practice writing any words that you made mistakes on again.

Some words have silent letters in them. All of the words below either contain a silent l or a silent n.

Remember: Say the word aloud, then say each letter aloud **as you write it** e.g. 'calm, c ... a ... l ... m'

If the sea is **calm** then there are no big waves in it.

_____ _____ _____ _____
_____ _____ _____ _____

If the weather is **balmy** then it is warm.

_____ _____ _____ _____
_____ _____ _____ _____

A **palm** tree has large green leaves.

_____ _____ _____ _____
_____ _____ _____ _____

A **calf** is a baby cow.

_____ _____ _____ _____
_____ _____ _____ _____

To get **half** of a number, you divide the number by two.

_____ _____ _____ _____
_____ _____ _____ _____

Chalk is used for writing on blackboards.

_____ _____ _____ _____
_____ _____ _____ _____

A **hymn** is a religious song.

_____ _____ _____ _____
_____ _____ _____ _____

A **column** is an upright support for a building that is cylinder-shaped.

_____ _____ _____ _____
_____ _____ _____ _____

A judge can **condemn** people to prison.

_____ _____ _____ _____
_____ _____ _____ _____

Solemn is another word for serious.

_____ _____ _____ _____
_____ _____ _____ _____

Now test yourself without looking at the words and **check for yourself** if you got them all right. Practice writing any words that you made mistakes on again.

Some words have silent letters in them. All of the words below contain a silent u.

Remember: Say the word aloud, then say each letter aloud **as you write it** e.g. 'guard, g ... u ... a ... r ... d'

A **guard** has the job of keeping someone or somewhere safe.

_____   _____   _____   _____
_____   _____   _____   _____

If you try to **guess** someone's age, you say how old you think he or she is.

_____   _____   _____   _____
_____   _____   _____   _____

A hotel **guest** is someone who is staying at the hotel.

_____   _____   _____   _____
_____   _____   _____   _____

A tourist **guide** tells you about a place.

_____   _____   _____   _____
_____   _____   _____   _____

A **guitar** is a type of string instrument.

_____   _____   _____   _____
_____   _____   _____   _____

If you do something wrong, you may feel **guilty** about it.

_____   _____   _____   _____
_____   _____   _____   _____

A **disguise** is used by someone to hide what they really look like.

_____   _____   _____   _____
_____   _____   _____   _____

A **guinea** is an old type of coin that we no longer use.

_____   _____   _____   _____
_____   _____   _____   _____

A **guardian** has the job of looking after a person or a place.

_____   _____   _____   _____
_____   _____   _____   _____

A new product comes with a **guarantee**, in case it stops working.

_____   _____   _____   _____
_____   _____   _____   _____

Now test yourself without looking at the words and **check for yourself** if you got them all right. Practice writing any words that you made mistakes on again.

Some words have silent letters in them. All of the words below contain either a silent h or a silent b.

Remember: Say the word aloud, then say each letter aloud **as you write it** e.g. 'rhyme, r ... h ... y ... m ... e'

The words bat and cat **rhyme**.
_____ _____ _____ _____
_____ _____ _____ _____

To be able to dance well, you need to hear the **rhythm** of the music.
_____ _____ _____ _____
_____ _____ _____ _____

A **rhombus** is a quadrilateral with four equal sides, but no right angles.
_____ _____ _____ _____
_____ _____ _____ _____

A **rhino** is a large animal with one or two horns on its snout.
_____ _____ _____ _____
_____ _____ _____ _____

Rhubarb is a plant with pink stalks that can be cooked as fruit.
_____ _____ _____ _____
_____ _____ _____ _____

If you **doubt** something, you are not sure if it is true.
_____ _____ _____ _____
_____ _____ _____ _____

A **debt** is money that is owed (borrowed, but not paid pack yet).
_____ _____ _____ _____
_____ _____ _____ _____

A **ghost** is a dead person who haunts a place.
_____ _____ _____ _____
_____ _____ _____ _____

A **ghoul** is an evil spirit.
_____ _____ _____ _____
_____ _____ _____ _____

Ghastly is another word for horrifying or terrible.
_____ _____ _____ _____
_____ _____ _____ _____

Now test yourself without looking at the words and **check for yourself** if you got them all right. Practice writing any words that you made mistakes on again.

All of the words below contain a silent letter.

Remember: Say the word aloud, then say each letter aloud **as you write it** e.g. 'island, i ... s ... l ... a ... n ... d'

An **island** *is land* in the middle of water.
_____ _____ _____ _____
_____ _____ _____ _____

A **sign** can tell you which direction you need to go in.
_____ _____ _____ _____
_____ _____ _____ _____

A carpenter will **build** things using wood.
_____ _____ _____ _____
_____ _____ _____ _____

You use your ears to **listen**.
_____ _____ _____ _____
_____ _____ _____ _____

A **psychic** is someone who can read people's minds.
_____ _____ _____ _____
_____ _____ _____ _____

A **sword** is like a large knife.
_____ _____ _____ _____
_____ _____ _____ _____

When someone asks you a question, you give an **answer**.
_____ _____ _____ _____
_____ _____ _____ _____

To **hasten** means to move or act quickly.
_____ _____ _____ _____
_____ _____ _____ _____

A **wreck** is what is left when a ship has sunk.
_____ _____ _____ _____
_____ _____ _____ _____

Your **wrist** is above your hand.
_____ _____ _____ _____
_____ _____ _____ _____

Now test yourself without looking at the words and <u>check for yourself</u> if you got them all right. Practice writing any words that you made mistakes on again.

All of the words below follow the spelling rule 'i before e, except after c'.

Remember: Say the word aloud, then say each letter aloud **as you write it** e.g. 'brief, b ... r ... i ... e ... f'

A **brief** amount of time is a short amount of time.

_____   _____   _____   _____
_____   _____   _____   _____

A **chief** is someone who is in charge.

_____   _____   _____   _____
_____   _____   _____   _____

Grief is what people feel when someone they are close to dies.

_____   _____   _____   _____
_____   _____   _____   _____

Someone who steals thing is a **thief**.

_____   _____   _____   _____
_____   _____   _____   _____

A farmer grows crops in a **field**.

_____   _____   _____   _____
_____   _____   _____   _____

A **shield** is used to block attacks in a fight.

_____   _____   _____   _____
_____   _____   _____   _____

Do you like to eat a **piece** of cake?

_____   _____   _____   _____
_____   _____   _____   _____

A **priest** leads mass in a church.

_____   _____   _____   _____
_____   _____   _____   _____

A **shriek** is a loud, high-pitched scream.

_____   _____   _____   _____
_____   _____   _____   _____

To **achieve** a goal means to complete it.

_____   _____   _____   _____
_____   _____   _____   _____

Now test yourself without looking at the words and **check for yourself** if you got them all right. Practice writing any words that you made mistakes on again.

Nearly all of the words below follow the spelling rule 'i before e, except after c'. However, the words protein, either and neither do not follow this rule.

Remember: Say the word aloud, then say each letter aloud **as you write it** e.g. 'believe, b … e … l … i … e … v … e'

Religious people **believe (be/lieve)** in God.

_____ _____ _____ _____
_____ _____ _____ _____

Christians have a **belief (be/lief)** that Jesus was the son of God.

_____ _____ _____ _____
_____ _____ _____ _____

Seize is another word for grab or take.

_____ _____ _____ _____
_____ _____ _____ _____

To **deceive (de/ceive)** someone means to trick them.

_____ _____ _____ _____
_____ _____ _____ _____

Do you prefer to give or to **receive (re/ceive)** presents?

_____ _____ _____ _____
_____ _____ _____ _____

How you **perceive (per/ceive)** something means how you see it.

_____ _____ _____ _____
_____ _____ _____ _____

The **ceiling (cei/ling)** is the top part of a room.

_____ _____ _____ _____
_____ _____ _____ _____

When you buy an item, you are given a **receipt (re/ceipt)** for it.

_____ _____ _____ _____
_____ _____ _____ _____

There is **protein (pro/tein)** in meat and in eggs.

_____ _____ _____ _____
_____ _____ _____ _____

You **either (ei/ther)** like Marmite or you do not like it.

_____ _____ _____ _____
_____ _____ _____ _____

Now test yourself without looking at the words and **check for yourself** if you got them all right. Practice writing any words that you made mistakes on again.

When a prefix ends with the same letter that the base words begins with, a hyphen is normally used. For example, co ends in o and operate starts with o.

Remember: Say the word aloud, then say each letter aloud **as you write it** e.g. 'co-operate, c ... o ... - ... o ... p ... e ... r ... a ... t ... e'

To **co-operate** with someone means to work with them.

_____ _____ _____ _____
_____ _____ _____ _____

To **co-ordinate** an event means to organise it.

_____ _____ _____ _____
_____ _____ _____ _____

To **co-author** a book means to write it with someone else.

_____ _____ _____ _____
_____ _____ _____ _____

If you **co-own** something, you share ownership of it with other people.

_____ _____ _____ _____
_____ _____ _____ _____

To **re-enter** a place means to come back into it.

_____ _____ _____ _____
_____ _____ _____ _____

To **re-educate** someone means to teach them something again.

_____ _____ _____ _____
_____ _____ _____ _____

To **re-examine** something means to look at it again.

_____ _____ _____ _____
_____ _____ _____ _____

To **re-evaluate** something means to think about it again.

_____ _____ _____ _____
_____ _____ _____ _____

To **re-energise** someone means to increase his or her energy levels.

_____ _____ _____ _____
_____ _____ _____ _____

To **re-explain** something means to explain it again.

_____ _____ _____ _____
_____ _____ _____ _____

Now test yourself without looking at the words and **check for yourself** if you got them all right. Practice writing any words that you made mistakes on again.

Name: _____   Date: _____   **-ard words**

The sound (urd) is often represented by the letters ard at the end of words of more than one syllable, like in the words below.

Remember: Say the word aloud, then say each letter aloud **as you write it** e.g. 'awkward, a ... w ... k ... w ... a ... r ... d'

If something is **awkward (aw/kward)**, it is tricky to do. _____
_____   _____   _____   _____

A **coward (cow/ard)** is someone who is often afraid. _____
_____   _____   _____   _____

You face **forward (for/ward)** when you walk. _____
_____   _____   _____   _____

If you reverse, you move in a **backward (back/ward)** direction. _____
_____   _____   _____   _____

A **lizard (liz/ard)** is a cold-blooded animal with scales. _____
_____   _____   _____   _____

A **wizard (wiz/ard)** is a man who can do magic. _____
_____   _____   _____   _____

In a **blizzard (bliz/zard)** heavy snow is blown by the wind. _____
_____   _____   _____   _____

A **leopard (leo/pard)** is a big cat with spots on its fur. _____
_____   _____   _____   _____

Mustard (mus/tard) is a dark yellow sauce. _____
_____   _____   _____   _____

Custard (cus/tard) is a yellow sauce that people can have with dessert. _____
_____   _____   _____   _____

Now test yourself without looking at the words and **check for yourself** if you got them all right. Practice writing any words that you made mistakes on again.

The words below are words that you need to learn in Year 5 and 6. Remember to break them into syllables when you try to spell them.

Remember: Say the word aloud, then say each letter aloud **as you write it** e.g. 'accommodate, a … c … c … o … m … m … o … d … a … t … e'

Accommodate (ac/com/mo/date) means to give someone a place to stay.

_____ _____ _____ _____
_____ _____ _____ _____

To **appreciate (ap/pre/ci/ate)** something means to be grateful for it.

_____ _____ _____ _____
_____ _____ _____ _____

To **communicate (com/mu/ni/cate)** means to give and receive information.

_____ _____ _____ _____
_____ _____ _____ _____

To **accompany (ac/com/pa/ny)** someone means to go with them.

_____ _____ _____ _____
_____ _____ _____ _____

According (ac/cor/ding) to the Bible, Adam and Eve were the first people.

_____ _____ _____ _____
_____ _____ _____ _____

A car is a type of **vehicle (ve/hi/cle)**.

_____ _____ _____ _____
_____ _____ _____ _____

A shark is an **aggressive (ag/gres/sive)** animal.

_____ _____ _____ _____
_____ _____ _____ _____

An **amateur (am/a/teur)** is someone who does not get paid.

_____ _____ _____ _____
_____ _____ _____ _____

If a file is **attached (at/ta/ched)** to an email, it is sent with it.

_____ _____ _____ _____
_____ _____ _____ _____

Average (a/ver/age) can mean satisfactory or normal.

_____ _____ _____ _____
_____ _____ _____ _____

Now test yourself without looking at the words and **check for yourself** if you got them all right. Practice writing any words that you made mistakes on again.

The words below are words that you need to learn in Year 5 and 6. Remember to break them into syllables when you try to spell them.

Remember: Say the word aloud, then say each letter aloud **as you write it** e.g. 'bargain, b ... a ... r ... g ... a ... i ... n'

Getting a **bargain (bar/gain)** means getting a good deal. _____

_____   _____   _____

A **bruise** is a blue and / or purple mark from an injury. _____

_____   _____   _____

A **category (cat/e/gor/y)** is a group for sorting things into. _____

_____   _____   _____

A **cemetery (cem/e/te/ry)** is a place where people are buried. _____

_____   _____   _____

People or teams try to win in a **competition (com/pe/ti/tion)**. _____

_____   _____   _____

Your **conscience (con/science)** makes you feel bad if you do wrong. _____

_____   _____   _____

You should be **conscious (con/scious)** of how you make other people feel. _____

_____   _____   _____

Controversy (con/tro/ver/sy) occurs when something offends people. _____

_____   _____   _____

A **convenience (con/ve/ni/ence)** shop is small and near people's houses. _____

_____   _____   _____

To **correspond (cor/re/spond)** with someone means to write to him or her. _____

_____   _____   _____

Now test yourself without looking at the words and **check for yourself** if you got them all right. Practice writing any words that you made mistakes on again.

The words below are words that you need to learn in Year 5 and 6. Remember to break them into syllables when you try to spell them.

Remember: Say the word aloud, then say each letter aloud **as you write it** e.g. 'criticise, c ... r ... i ... t ... i ... c ... i ... s ... e'

To **criticise (cri/ti/cise)** a person is to say what he or she has done badly.
_____ _____ _____ _____
_____ _____ _____ _____

To have **curiosity (cu/ri/o/si/ty)** means to want to find out more.
_____ _____ _____ _____
_____ _____ _____ _____

To **develop (de/ve/lop)** can mean to grow or to improve.
_____ _____ _____ _____
_____ _____ _____ _____

A **disastrous (di/sas/trous)** event is a very bad and very serious one.
_____ _____ _____ _____
_____ _____ _____ _____

Mums can **embarass (em/ba/rass)** older boys by giving them a kiss.
_____ _____ _____ _____
_____ _____ _____ _____

An animal's **environment (en/vi/ron/ment)** is where it lives.
_____ _____ _____ _____
_____ _____ _____ _____

You should be **especially (e/spe/cial/ly)** nice to your mum on her birthday.
_____ _____ _____ _____
_____ _____ _____ _____

If you **exaggerate (ex/ag/ger/ate)** you talk up what you have done.
_____ _____ _____ _____
_____ _____ _____ _____

Some people believe in the **existence (ex/is/tence)** of aliens.
_____ _____ _____ _____
_____ _____ _____ _____

You need to have an **explanation (ex/pla/na/tion)** for not doing homework.
_____ _____ _____ _____
_____ _____ _____ _____

Now test yourself without looking at the words and <u>**check for yourself**</u> if you got them all right. Practice writing any words that you made mistakes on again.

The words below are words that you need to learn in Year 5 and 6. Remember to break them into syllables when you try to spell them.

Remember: Say the word aloud, then say each letter aloud **as you write it** e.g. 'foreign, f … o … r … e … i … g … n'

To be **foreign (fo/reign)** means to come from another country.
_____ _____ _____ _____
_____ _____ _____ _____

Forty (for/ty) comes after thirty-nine.
_____ _____ _____ _____
_____ _____ _____ _____

To do something **frequently (fre/quent/ly)** means to do it often.
_____ _____ _____ _____
_____ _____ _____ _____

The **government (go/vern/ment)** makes the laws for the country.
_____ _____ _____ _____
_____ _____ _____ _____

To **harass (ha/rass)** someone means to bother them repeatedly.
_____ _____ _____ _____
_____ _____ _____ _____

A **hindrance (hin/drance)** is something that gets in the way.
_____ _____ _____ _____
_____ _____ _____ _____

Your passport is proof of your **identity (i/den/ti/ty)**.
_____ _____ _____ _____
_____ _____ _____ _____

The **immediate (im/me/di/ate)** problem is the first one that needs fixing.
_____ _____ _____ _____
_____ _____ _____ _____

An **individual (in/di/vi/du/al)** is one person.
_____ _____ _____ _____
_____ _____ _____ _____

To **interfere (in/ter/fere)** means to get involved when you should not do.
_____ _____ _____ _____
_____ _____ _____ _____

Now test yourself without looking at the words and <u>check for yourself</u> if you got them all right. Practice writing any words that you made mistakes on again.

The words below are words that you need to learn in Year 5 and 6. Remember to break them into syllables when you try to spell them.

Remember: Say the word aloud, then say each letter aloud **as you write it** e.g. 'interrupt, i ... n ... t ... e ... r ... r ... u ... p ... t'

To **interrupt (in/ter/rupt)** means to talk when someone else is talking.
_____ _____ _____ _____
_____ _____ _____ _____

English is the main **language (lan/guage)** of the UK.
_____ _____ _____ _____
_____ _____ _____ _____

Leisure (lei/sure) activities are things that you do in your free time.
_____ _____ _____ _____
_____ _____ _____ _____

Lightning (light/ning) is the flashes of light that can happen in a storm.
_____ _____ _____ _____
_____ _____ _____ _____

Marvellous (mar/vel/lous) means really wonderful.
_____ _____ _____ _____
_____ _____ _____ _____

A **mischievous (mis/chie/vous)** child is one that is always up to something.
_____ _____ _____ _____
_____ _____ _____ _____

Your thigh **muscle (mu/scle)** is at the top of your leg.
_____ _____ _____ _____
_____ _____ _____ _____

A **neighbour (neigh/bour)** is someone who lives next door.
_____ _____ _____ _____
_____ _____ _____ _____

To **occupy (oc/cu/py)** a seat means to sit in it.
_____ _____ _____ _____
_____ _____ _____ _____

A **yacht** is a type of sailing boat.
_____ _____ _____ _____
_____ _____ _____ _____

Now test yourself without looking at the words and **check for yourself** if you got them all right. Practice writing any words that you made mistakes on again.

The words below are words that you need to learn in Year 5 and 6. Remember to break them into syllables when you try to spell them.

Remember: Say the word aloud, then say each letter aloud **as you write it** e.g. 'occur, o ... c ... c ... u ... r'

Occur (oc/cur) is another word for happen.

_____   _____   _____   _____

_____   _____   _____   _____

Going to school is an **opportunity (op/por/tu/ni/ty)** to learn more.

_____   _____   _____   _____

Parliament (par/lia/ment) is where the laws of the UK are made.

_____   _____   _____   _____

To **persuade (per/suade)** people means to change their minds.

_____   _____   _____   _____

PE is an acronym for **physical (phy/si/cal)** education.

_____   _____   _____   _____

A **prejudice (pre/ju/dice)** is a negative belief about a group of people.

_____   _____   _____   _____

A **privilege (pri/vi/lege)** is a special honour or treat.

_____   _____   _____   _____

A **profession (pro/fes/sion)** is a job that you need training for.

_____   _____   _____   _____

What is your favourite TV **programme (pro/gramme)**?

_____   _____   _____   _____

Pronunciation (pro/nun/ci/a/tion) is about how you say words.

_____   _____   _____   _____

Now test yourself without looking at the words and **check for yourself** if you got them all right. Practice writing any words that you made mistakes on again.

The words below are words that you need to learn in Year 5 and 6. Remember to break them into syllables when you try to spell them.

Remember: Say the word aloud, then say each letter aloud **as you write it** e.g. 'queue, q ... u ... e ... u ... e'

A **queue** is a line of people waiting to do something.
_____   _____   _____   _____
_____   _____   _____   _____

To **recognise (re/cog/nise)** people you need to know what they look like.
_____   _____   _____   _____

If you **recommend (rec/om/mend)** a film, you tell someone to watch it.
_____   _____   _____   _____
_____   _____   _____   _____

A **restaurant (re/stau/rant)** is a place where you pay for food and eat it.
_____   _____   _____   _____

Making a **sacrifice (sa/cri/fice)** means giving up something that you like.
_____   _____   _____   _____

Your **shoulder (shoul/der)** is at the top of your arm.
_____   _____   _____   _____

Sincere (sin/cere) is another word for genuine and honest.
_____   _____   _____   _____
_____   _____   _____   _____

A **soldier (sol/dier)** works in the army.
_____   _____   _____   _____

Your **stomach (sto/mach)** is where your food goes when you swallow it.
_____   _____   _____   _____

To **suggest (sug/gest)** something means that you advise someone to do it.
_____   _____   _____   _____
_____   _____   _____   _____

Now test yourself without looking at the words and **check for yourself** if you got them all right. Practice writing any words that you made mistakes on again.

The words below are words that you need to learn in Year 5 and 6. Remember to break them into syllables when you try to spell them.

Remember: Say the word aloud, then say each letter aloud **as you write it** e.g. 'symbol, s ... y ... m ... b ... o ... l'

A dove is a **symbol (sym/bol)** of peace.
_____   _____   _____   _____
_____   _____   _____   _____

A security **system (sys/tem)** needs to keep a place safe.
_____   _____   _____   _____

The **temperature (tem/per/a/ture)** tells you how hot or how cold it is.
_____   _____   _____   _____

The **twelfth** day of the month comes after the eleventh day of the month.
_____   _____   _____   _____

Someone who has a **variety (va/ri/e/ty)** of interests likes different things.
_____   _____   _____   _____

A **community (com/mu/ni/ty)** is a group of people.
_____   _____   _____   _____

A **committee (com/mit/tee)** is a group of people who make decisions.
_____   _____   _____   _____

To be **determined (de/ter/mined)** means to really try hard.
_____   _____   _____   _____

You need to be properly **equipped (e/quip/ped)** to go mountain climbing.
_____   _____   _____   _____

You need the right **equipment (e/quip/ment)** to go mountain climbing.
_____   _____   _____   _____

Now test yourself without looking at the words and **check for yourself** if you got them all right. Practice writing any words that you made mistakes on again.

© www.SaveTeachersSundays.com 2013

The sound (ut) is often represented by the letters ate when it comes at the end of words of more than one syllable, like in the words below.

Remember: Say the word aloud, then say each letter aloud **as you write it** e.g. 'private, p ... r ... i ... v ... a ... t ... e'

People get dressed and undressed in **private (pri/vate)**.
_____   _____   _____   _____
_____   _____   _____   _____

To be **desperate (des/per/ate)** for something means to really need it.
_____   _____   _____   _____
_____   _____   _____   _____

Crocodiles and alligators are **separate (se/per/ate)** species.
_____   _____   _____   _____
_____   _____   _____   _____

A **certificate (cer/ti/fi/cate)** is a paper or cardboard award.
_____   _____   _____   _____
_____   _____   _____   _____

Chocolate (cho/co/late) is usually brown and sweet.
_____   _____   _____   _____
_____   _____   _____   _____

A **graduate (gra/du/ate)** is someone who has finished a university course.
_____   _____   _____   _____
_____   _____   _____   _____

Adequate (a/de/quate) is another word for satisfactory or OK.
_____   _____   _____   _____
_____   _____   _____   _____

To be **accurate (ac/cu/rate)** when shooting means to hit the target.
_____   _____   _____   _____
_____   _____   _____   _____

The **ultimate (ul/ti/mate)** roller-coaster is the best one.
_____   _____   _____   _____
_____   _____   _____   _____

Elaborate (e/la/bo/rate) means not straightforward.
_____   _____   _____   _____
_____   _____   _____   _____

Now test yourself without looking at the words and **check for yourself** if you got them all right. Practice writing any words that you made mistakes on again.

The sound (it) can be represented by the letters ite or by the letters it when it comes at the end of words of more than one syllable, like in the words below.

Remember: Say the word aloud, then say each letter aloud **as you write it** e.g. 'opposite, o ... p ... p ... o ... s ... i ... t ... e'

Black is the **opposite (op/po/site)** of white.

_____   _____   _____   _____
_____   _____   _____   _____

To be **definite (de/fi/nite)** about something means to be very sure of it.

_____   _____   _____   _____
_____   _____   _____   _____

Granite (gra/nite) is a tough igneous rock.

_____   _____   _____   _____
_____   _____   _____   _____

An **infinite (in/fi/nite)** amount cannot be counted or measured.

_____   _____   _____   _____
_____   _____   _____   _____

Exquisite (ex/qui/site) means beautiful or really excellent.

_____   _____   _____   _____
_____   _____   _____   _____

A **hypocrite (hy/po/crite)** says one thing, but does another.

_____   _____   _____   _____
_____   _____   _____   _____

One **benefit (be/ne/fit)** of exercise is that it makes your muscles strong.

_____   _____   _____   _____
_____   _____   _____   _____

To give someone **credit (cre/dit)** is to say that he or she did well.

_____   _____   _____   _____
_____   _____   _____   _____

To have a strong **spirit (spi/rit)** means that you do not give up easily.

_____   _____   _____   _____
_____   _____   _____   _____

To **commit (com/mit)** to something means to really do your best at it.

_____   _____   _____   _____
_____   _____   _____   _____

Now test yourself without looking at the words and **check for yourself** if you got them all right. Practice writing any words that you made mistakes on again.

The sound (in) is often represented by the letters ine when it comes at the end of words of more than one syllable, like in the words below.

Remember: Say the word aloud, then say each letter aloud **as you write it** e.g. 'engine, e ... n ... g ... i ... n ... e'

A car needs an **engine (en/gine)** so that it can move.
_____ _____ _____ _____
_____ _____ _____ _____

If there is no food, there is a **famine (fa/mine)**.
_____ _____ _____ _____
_____ _____ _____ _____

To **determine (de/ter/mine)** something means to work it out.
_____ _____ _____ _____
_____ _____ _____ _____

An athlete needs to have **discipline (di/sci/pline)** to train well.
_____ _____ _____ _____
_____ _____ _____ _____

When you visit a doctor, he or she will **examine (ex/a/mine)** you.
_____ _____ _____ _____
_____ _____ _____ _____

Genuine (gen/u/ine) means real or not fake.
_____ _____ _____ _____
_____ _____ _____ _____

A **heroine (he/ro/ine)** is a female hero.
_____ _____ _____ _____
_____ _____ _____ _____

To **imagine (i/ma/gine)** something means to picture it in your mind.
_____ _____ _____ _____
_____ _____ _____ _____

Perfume and dresses are **feminine (fe/mi/nine)**.
_____ _____ _____ _____
_____ _____ _____ _____

Aftershave and beards are **masculine (ma/scu/line)**.
_____ _____ _____ _____
_____ _____ _____ _____

Now test yourself without looking at the words and **check for yourself** if you got them all right. Practice writing any words that you made mistakes on again.

The sound (een) is sometimes represented by the letters ine when it comes at the end of words of more than one syllable, like in the words below.

Remember: Say the word aloud, then say each letter aloud **as you write it** e.g. 'vaccine, v ... a ... c ... c ... i ... n ... e'

A **vaccine (vac/cine)** for a disease stops you getting that disease.

_____ _____ _____ _____
_____ _____ _____ _____

Pristine (pri/stine) means in perfect condition.

_____ _____ _____ _____
_____ _____ _____ _____

A **routine (rou/tine)** is done the same way each time it is done.

_____ _____ _____ _____
_____ _____ _____ _____

A coffee **machine (ma/chine)** makes coffee.

_____ _____ _____ _____
_____ _____ _____ _____

A **ravine (ra/vine)** is a deep, narrow valley.

_____ _____ _____ _____
_____ _____ _____ _____

A **submarine (sub/ma/rine)** is a vessel that can go under water.

_____ _____ _____ _____
_____ _____ _____ _____

A **magazine (ma/ga/zine)** is a weekly or monthly book on a topic.

_____ _____ _____ _____
_____ _____ _____ _____

A **trampoline (tram/po/line)** allows you to jump higher than normal.

_____ _____ _____ _____
_____ _____ _____ _____

Cuisine (cui/sine) means high quality food.

_____ _____ _____ _____
_____ _____ _____ _____

Caffeine (caf/feine) is found in coffee and helps you to stay awake.

_____ _____ _____ _____
_____ _____ _____ _____

Now test yourself without looking at the words and **check for yourself** if you got them all right. Practice writing any words that you made mistakes on again.

A number of words end in the letters ary, like the words below.

Remember: Say the word aloud, then say each letter aloud **as you write it** e.g. 'contrary, c ... o ... n ... t ... r ... a ... r ... y'

Contrary (con/tra/ry) means miserable and argumentative.
_____ _____ _____ _____
_____ _____ _____ _____

You can look up the meaning of words in a **dictionary (dic/tion/a/ry)**.
_____ _____ _____ _____
_____ _____ _____ _____

A **secretary (se/cre/ta/ry)** helps to organise his or her boss's schedule.
_____ _____ _____ _____
_____ _____ _____ _____

You can borrow books from a **library (li/bra/ry)**.
_____ _____ _____ _____
_____ _____ _____ _____

If something is **necessary (ne/ces/sa/ry)** that means that it is needed.
_____ _____ _____ _____
_____ _____ _____ _____

Red, green and blue are the **primary (pri/ma/ry)** colours.
_____ _____ _____ _____
_____ _____ _____ _____

You go to **secondary (se/con/da/ry)** school when you leave primary school.
_____ _____ _____ _____
_____ _____ _____ _____

Ordinary (or/di/na/ry) is another word for usual or normal.
_____ _____ _____ _____
_____ _____ _____ _____

If a job is **temporary (tem/po/ra/ry)**, it is only for a set amount of time.
_____ _____ _____ _____
_____ _____ _____ _____

A **diary (di/a/ry)** is a book that you write in each day.
_____ _____ _____ _____
_____ _____ _____ _____

Now test yourself without looking at the words and **check for yourself** if you got them all right. Practice writing any words that you made mistakes on again.

The sound (ur) is most often represented by the letters er at the end of words of more than one syllable, like in the words below.

Remember: Say the word aloud, then say each letter aloud **as you write it** e.g. 'number, n ... u ... m ... b ... e ... r'

Do you have a lucky **number (num/ber)?**
_____ _____ _____ _____
_____ _____ _____ _____

To get into a club, you need to be a **member (mem/ber).**
_____ _____ _____ _____
_____ _____ _____ _____

To **transfer (trans/fer)** something means to move it.
_____ _____ _____ _____
_____ _____ _____ _____

If a friend is upset, you might try to find out what's the **matter (mat/ter).**
_____ _____ _____ _____

You need to decide **whether (whe/ther)** to try your best or not.
_____ _____ _____ _____
_____ _____ _____ _____

If you hear **laughter (laugh/ter),** you know people are having fun.
_____ _____ _____ _____
_____ _____ _____ _____

A **chapter (chap/ter)** is one part of a book.
_____ _____ _____ _____
_____ _____ _____ _____

PC can stand for personal **computer (com/pu/ter).**
_____ _____ _____ _____
_____ _____ _____ _____

The whole school is **altogether (al/to/ge/ther)** at assembly time.
_____ _____ _____ _____
_____ _____ _____ _____

A **daughter (daugh/ter)** is a female child.
_____ _____ _____ _____
_____ _____ _____ _____

Now test yourself without looking at the words and **check for yourself** if you got them all right. Practice writing any words that you made mistakes on again.

The sound (ur) is sometimes represented by the letters ar at the end of words of more than one syllable, like in the words below.

Remember: Say the word aloud, then say each letter aloud **as you write it** e.g. 'cellar, c ... e ... l ... l ... a ... r'

A **cellar (cel/lar)** is a part of a building that is underground.
_____ _____ _____ _____
_____ _____ _____ _____

A **collar (col/lar)** is the top part of a shirt that can be bent over.
_____ _____ _____ _____
_____ _____ _____ _____

A **beggar (beg/gar)** asks for money without doing anything to earn it.
_____ _____ _____ _____
_____ _____ _____ _____

A **burglar (bur/glar)** breaks into people's homes and steals things.
_____ _____ _____ _____
_____ _____ _____ _____

Polar (po/lar) bears live in cold places.
_____ _____ _____ _____
_____ _____ _____ _____

Solar (so/lar) power comes from the sun.
_____ _____ _____ _____
_____ _____ _____ _____

Do you like **vinegar (vin/e/gar)** on your chips?
_____ _____ _____ _____
_____ _____ _____ _____

A **scholar (scho/lar)** is someone who studies one thing a lot.
_____ _____ _____ _____
_____ _____ _____ _____

Friends are **familiar (fa/mi/li/ar)** with each other.
_____ _____ _____ _____
_____ _____ _____ _____

If two things are **similar (si/mi/lar)**, then they are almost the same.
_____ _____ _____ _____
_____ _____ _____ _____

Now test yourself without looking at the words and **check for yourself** if you got them all right. Practice writing any words that you made mistakes on again.

The sound (is) is most often represented by the letters ice at the end of words of more than one syllable, like in the words below.

Remember: Say the word aloud, then say each letter aloud **as you write it** e.g. 'office, o ... f ... f ... i ... c ... e'

Some people work in an **office (of/fice)** with computers and phones.
_____ _____ _____ _____
_____ _____ _____ _____

A **hospice (hos/pice)** looks after people who are very sick.
_____ _____ _____ _____
_____ _____ _____ _____

The courts are in charge of **justice (jus/tice)**.
_____ _____ _____ _____
_____ _____ _____ _____

What time is football **practice (prac/tice)**?
_____ _____ _____ _____
_____ _____ _____ _____

A hotel should provide good **service (ser/vice)** to its guests.
_____ _____ _____ _____
_____ _____ _____ _____

To **notice (no/tice)** something means to see or to spot it.
_____ _____ _____ _____
_____ _____ _____ _____

If you make a **promise (pro/mise)**, you should keep it.
_____ _____ _____ _____
_____ _____ _____ _____

To become good at a skill you need to **practise (prac/tise)** it a lot.
_____ _____ _____ _____
_____ _____ _____ _____

To play **tennis (ten/nis)** you need a racquet and a ball.
_____ _____ _____ _____
_____ _____ _____ _____

If an animal is a **menace (men/ace)**, then it is dangerous.
_____ _____ _____ _____
_____ _____ _____ _____

Now test yourself without looking at the words and **check for yourself** if you got them all right. Practice writing any words that you made mistakes on again.

The sound (shun) is most often represented by the letters tion at the end of words, like in the words below.

Remember: Say the word aloud, then say each letter aloud **as you write it** e.g. 'condition, c ... o ... n ... d ... i ... t ... i ... o ... n'

If you are in good **condition (con/di/tion)** that means that you are fit.
_____   _____   _____   _____
_____   _____   _____   _____

In an **election (e/lec/tion)** you vote for people or for parties.
_____   _____   _____   _____
_____   _____   _____   _____

In sport the **opposition (op/po/si/tion)** are the people that you try to beat.
_____   _____   _____   _____
_____   _____   _____   _____

When you have a problem, you need a **solution (so/lu/tion)** to it.
_____   _____   _____   _____
_____   _____   _____   _____

Making a **contribution (con/tri/bu/tion)** to charity means giving something.
_____   _____   _____   _____
_____   _____   _____   _____

An **introduction (in/tro/duc/tion)** comes at the start of a piece of writing.
_____   _____   _____   _____
_____   _____   _____   _____

Royal Mail are in charge of the **distribution (dis/tri/bu/tion)** of post.
_____   _____   _____   _____
_____   _____   _____   _____

People go to an art **exhibition (ex/hi/bi/tion)** to see artwork.
_____   _____   _____   _____
_____   _____   _____   _____

The **definition (de/fi/ni/tion)** of a word tells you what it means.
_____   _____   _____   _____
_____   _____   _____   _____

If you have a good **intention (in/ten/tion)**, you want to do something good.
_____   _____   _____   _____
_____   _____   _____   _____

Now test yourself without looking at the words and <u>**check for yourself**</u> if you got them all right. Practice writing any words that you made mistakes on again.

A number of words end in the letters ation, like the words below.

Remember: Say the word aloud, then say each letter aloud **as you write it** e.g. 'education, e ... d ... u ... c ... a ... t ... i ... o ... n'

You go to school to get an **education (e/du/ca/tion)**.
_____ _____ _____ _____
_____ _____ _____ _____

The **population (po/pu/la/tion)** is the number of people that live in a place.
_____ _____ _____ _____

If you are badly injured, you may need an **operation (o/per/a/tion)** to fix it.
_____ _____ _____ _____

Trains stop to let people on and off at a **station (sta/tion)**.
_____ _____ _____ _____
_____ _____ _____ _____

Communication (com/mu/ni/ca/tion) means giving and receiving information.
_____ _____ _____ _____

To give something **consideration (con/si/der/a/tion)** is to think about it.
_____ _____ _____ _____

Power stations are used for the **generation (ge/ner/a/tion)** of electricity.
_____ _____ _____ _____

A science **investigation (in/ve/sti/ga/tion)** tests out an idea.
_____ _____ _____ _____

You need an **explanation (ex/pla/na/tion)** for not doing your homework.
_____ _____ _____ _____

Your **location (lo/ca/tion)** is where you are.
_____ _____ _____ _____

Now test yourself without looking at the words and **check for yourself** if you got them all right. Practice writing any words that you made mistakes on again.

Homophones and Confusable Words 1

For each pair of words, write two sentences, with each sentence including one of the words.

Look them up in the dictionary if you need to.

Example:

advice / advise

The best <u>advice</u> I can give you is to do your best.

I would <u>advise</u> you to say sorry.

1) advice / advise

2) devi<u>c</u>e / devi<u>s</u>e

3) licen<u>c</u>e / licen<u>s</u>e

4) practi<u>c</u>e / practi<u>s</u>e

5) <u>a</u>isle / isle

6) aloud / allowed

7) <u>a</u>ffect / <u>e</u>ffect

8) alt<u>a</u>r / alt<u>e</u>r

9) as<u>c</u>ent / as<u>s</u>ent

10) bridal / bridle

11) cereal / serial

The sound (shun) is sometimes represented by the letters sion at the end of words, like in the words below.

Remember: Say the word aloud, then say each letter aloud **as you write it** e.g. 'provision, p ... r ... o ... v ... i ... s ... i ... o ... n'

Does your school have **provision (pro/vi/sion)** for afterschool clubs?
_____ _____ _____ _____
_____ _____ _____ _____

Someone who is blind has lost his or her **vision (vi/sion)**.
_____ _____ _____ _____
_____ _____ _____ _____

If a house has an **extension (ex/ten/sion)**, there has been a part added to it.
_____ _____ _____ _____

Pumping air into a balloon causes its **expansion (ex/pan/sion)**.
_____ _____ _____ _____

Soil **erosion (e/ro/sion)** is when soil gets washed away or blown away.
_____ _____ _____ _____
_____ _____ _____ _____

Precision (pre/ci/sion) is another word for accuracy.
_____ _____ _____ _____

An **illusion (il/lu/sion)** is something that seems real, even though it isn't.
_____ _____ _____ _____
_____ _____ _____ _____

A **mansion (man/sion)** is a huge house.
_____ _____ _____ _____

A **collision (col/li/sion)** happens when things smash into each other.
_____ _____ _____ _____
_____ _____ _____ _____

If a bus is on a **diversion (di/ver/sion)**, it does not follow its usual route.
_____ _____ _____ _____
_____ _____ _____ _____

Now test yourself without looking at the words and **check for yourself** if you got them all right. Practice writing any words that you made mistakes on again.

Homophones and Confusable Words 2

For each pair of words, write two sentences, with each sentence including one of the words.

Look them up in the dictionary if you need to.

Example:

compliment / complement

Make sure you <u>compliment</u> mum on her new hair style.

Cheese is a good <u>complement</u> to crackers.

---

1) compl<u>i</u>ment / compl<u>e</u>ment

2) descent / dissent

3) disinterested / uninterested

4) draft / draught

5) de<u>s</u>ert / de<u>ss</u>ert

6) prophe<u>c</u>y / prophe<u>s</u>y

7) eligible / illegible

8) eliminate / illuminate

9) farther / father

10) guessed / guest

The sound (shun) is sometimes represented by the letters ssion at the end of words, like in the words below.

Remember: Say the word aloud, then say each letter aloud **as you write it** e.g. 'passion, p ... a ... s ... s ... i ... o ... n'

To have a **passion (pa/ssion)** for something means to really care about it.

_____   _____   _____   _____

_____   _____   _____   _____

If you push your hand into clay, it leaves an **impression (im/pre/ssion)**.

_____   _____   _____   _____

_____   _____   _____   _____

The **admission (ad/mi/ssion)** price for an event means how much it is to get in.

_____   _____   _____   _____

_____   _____   _____   _____

The **emission (e/mis/ssion)** from a car exhaust includes carbon dioxide.

_____   _____   _____   _____

An animal shows **aggression (ag/gre/ssion)** if it feels threatened.

_____   _____   _____   _____

_____   _____   _____   _____

A **concession (con/ce/ssion)** is a reduced price for older or younger people.

_____   _____   _____   _____

_____   _____   _____   _____

A **procession (pro/ce/ssion)** is a line of people or vehicles moving forward.

_____   _____   _____   _____

_____   _____   _____   _____

A **confession (con/fe/ssion)** is when someone admits doing something bad.

_____   _____   _____   _____

_____   _____   _____   _____

To have an **obsession (ob/se/ssion)** is to focus too much on something.

_____   _____   _____   _____

_____   _____   _____   _____

A **cushion (cu/shion)** makes a seat softer to sit on.   _____

_____   _____   _____   _____

Now test yourself without looking at the words and **check for yourself** if you got them all right. Practice writing any words that you made mistakes on again.

Homophones and Confusable Words 3

For each pair of words, write two sentences, with each sentence including one of the words.

Look them up in the dictionary if you need to.

> Example:
>
> heard / herd
>
> Have you <u>heard</u> the news?
>
> A <u>herd</u> of sheep are blocking the road.

1) he<u>a</u>rd / herd

2) led / le<u>a</u>d

3) morning / mo<u>u</u>rning

4) past / passed

5) precede / proceed

6) principal / principle

7) profit / prophet

8) station<u>a</u>ry / station<u>e</u>ry

9) ste<u>a</u>l / ste<u>e</u>l

10) wary / weary

11) who's / whose

12) current / currant

The sound (chu) is usually represented by the letters ture at the end of words. The sound (shun) is represented by the letters cian in job names.

Remember: Say the word aloud, then say each letter aloud **as you write it** e.g. 'fracture, f ... r ... a ... c ... t ... u ... r ... e'

A **fracture (frac/ture)** is a break in a bone.

_____   _____   _____   _____
_____   _____   _____   _____

In sport a **fixture (fix/ture)** is a match between two people or teams.

_____   _____   _____   _____
_____   _____   _____   _____

A **gesture (ges/ture)** is a movement that shows an emotion.

_____   _____   _____   _____
_____   _____   _____   _____

To **nurture (nur/ture)** a plant means to look after it so that it grows.

_____   _____   _____   _____
_____   _____   _____   _____

Moisture (mois/ture) is another word for wetness.

_____   _____   _____   _____
_____   _____   _____   _____

A **physician (phy/si/cian)** is another name for a doctor.

_____   _____   _____   _____
_____   _____   _____   _____

A **technician (tech/ni/cian)** is someone who works in a laboratory.

_____   _____   _____   _____
_____   _____   _____   _____

A **mathematician (math/e/ma/ti/cian)** has a job involving maths.

_____   _____   _____   _____
_____   _____   _____   _____

A **statistician (sta/ti/sti/cian)** works with statistics.

_____   _____   _____   _____
_____   _____   _____   _____

A **paediatrician (pae/di/a/tri/cian)** is a doctor who helps children.

_____   _____   _____   _____
_____   _____   _____   _____

Now test yourself without looking at the words and **check for yourself** if you got them all right. Practice writing any words that you made mistakes on again.

The sound (us) is usually represented by the letters **ous** at the end of **adjectives** of more than one syllable, like in the words below.

Remember: Say the word aloud, then say each letter aloud **as you write it** e.g. 'odious, o ... d ... i ... o ... u ... s'

Odious (o/di/ous) is another word for hateful or disgusting.

_____ _____ _____ _____
_____ _____ _____ _____

If a rock is **porous (por/ous)**, it has holes in it that let water through.

_____ _____ _____ _____
_____ _____ _____ _____

Aqueous (a/que/ous) is another word for watery.

_____ _____ _____ _____
_____ _____ _____ _____

If something is **arduous (ar/du/ous)**, then it is difficult and tiring to do.

_____ _____ _____ _____
_____ _____ _____ _____

To be **callous (cal/lous)** means to have no concern for other people.

_____ _____ _____ _____
_____ _____ _____ _____

A **copious (co/pi/ous)** amount is a very large amount.

_____ _____ _____ _____
_____ _____ _____ _____

Heinous (hei/nous) means really evil.

_____ _____ _____ _____
_____ _____ _____ _____

Igneous (ig/ne/ous) rocks are formed when lava cools down.

_____ _____ _____ _____
_____ _____ _____ _____

To be **jealous (jea/lous)** is to be unhappy because of what someone else has.

_____ _____ _____ _____
_____ _____ _____ _____

To have an **ominous (o/mi/nous)** feeling means you expect something bad.

_____ _____ _____ _____
_____ _____ _____ _____

Now test yourself without looking at the words and **check for yourself** if you got them all right. Practice writing any words that you made mistakes on again.

The sound (us) is usually represented by the letters **us** at the end of **nouns** of more than one syllable, like in the words below.

Remember: Say the word aloud, then say each letter aloud **as you write it** e.g. 'focus, f … o … c … u … s'

To **focus (fo/cus)** on something means to concentrate on it.

_____ _____ _____ _____
_____ _____ _____ _____

A person's **status (sta/tus)** is about how important he or she is.

_____ _____ _____ _____
_____ _____ _____ _____

A **virus (vi/rus)** can cause disease, such as flu.

_____ _____ _____ _____
_____ _____ _____ _____

If a worker gets a **bonus (bo/nus)**, he or she gets some extra money.

_____ _____ _____ _____
_____ _____ _____ _____

Lemons and limes are types of **citrus (cit/rus)** fruit.

_____ _____ _____ _____
_____ _____ _____ _____

A **census (cen/sus)** finds out information about the people in a country.

_____ _____ _____ _____
_____ _____ _____ _____

The **chorus (cho/rus)** of a song is the part that is repeated.

_____ _____ _____ _____
_____ _____ _____ _____

Surplus (sur/plus) means more than is needed.

_____ _____ _____ _____
_____ _____ _____ _____

If there is **consensus (con/sen/sus)** that means that everyone agrees.

_____ _____ _____ _____
_____ _____ _____ _____

Mushrooms are a type of **fungus (fun/gus)**.

_____ _____ _____ _____
_____ _____ _____ _____

Now test yourself without looking at the words and **check for yourself** if you got them all right. Practice writing any words that you made mistakes on again.

In the words below the letters ou are used to represent either the long (oo) sound or the long (o) sound.

Remember: Say the word aloud, then say each letter aloud **as you write it** e.g. 'soup, s ... o ... u ... p'

Soup is liquid food.
_____ _____ _____ _____
_____ _____ _____ _____

A **group** of people means more than one person.
_____ _____ _____ _____
_____ _____ _____ _____

A bus travels the same **route** every day.
_____ _____ _____ _____
_____ _____ _____ _____

A **wound** is another name for an injury.
_____ _____ _____ _____
_____ _____ _____ _____

Your **youth** is the time when you are young.
_____ _____ _____ _____
_____ _____ _____ _____

A **coupon** allows you to get money off or to get a special offer.
_____ _____ _____ _____
_____ _____ _____ _____

To **mould** clay means to give it shape.
_____ _____ _____ _____
_____ _____ _____ _____

A **boulder** is a large rock.
_____ _____ _____ _____
_____ _____ _____ _____

A fire will **smoulder** just before it goes out.
_____ _____ _____ _____
_____ _____ _____ _____

Most religious people believe you have a **soul** that survives when you die.
_____ _____ _____ _____
_____ _____ _____ _____

Now test yourself without looking at the words and **check for yourself** if you got them all right. Practice writing any words that you made mistakes on again.

Very few words use the letters eu to represent the long (u) sound.
Very few words use the letters ch to represent the (sh) sound.

Remember: Say the word aloud, then say each letter aloud **as you write it** e.g.
'Europe, E ... u ... r ... o ... p ... e'

The UK is part of the continent of **Europe (Eu/rope)**.
_____ _____ _____ _____
_____ _____ _____ _____

A **feud** is an argument that has gone on for a very long time.
_____ _____ _____ _____
_____ _____ _____ _____

A referee needs to be **neutral (neu/tral)** (to not favour either side).
_____ _____ _____ _____
_____ _____ _____ _____

To feel **euphoria (eu/pho/ri/a)** means to feel extremely happy.
_____ _____ _____ _____
_____ _____ _____ _____

A **euphemism (eu/phe/mi/sm)** is a nice way of saying something unpleasant.
_____ _____ _____ _____
_____ _____ _____ _____

Pneumonia (pneu/mo/ni/a) is a disease that causes problems with lungs.
_____ _____ _____ _____
_____ _____ _____ _____

A **chef** cooks meals for a living.
_____ _____ _____ _____
_____ _____ _____ _____

A **chalet (cha/let)** is a small wooden house.
_____ _____ _____ _____
_____ _____ _____ _____

A **brochure (bro/chure)** is a book that advertises a place or a service.
_____ _____ _____ _____
_____ _____ _____ _____

People use a **parachute (pa/ra/chute)** when they jump from a plane.
_____ _____ _____ _____
_____ _____ _____ _____

Now test yourself without looking at the words and <u>**check for yourself**</u> if you got
them all right. Practice writing any words that you made mistakes on again.

Very few words use the y-e pattern to represent the long (i) sound, like in the words below.

Remember: Say the word aloud, then say each letter aloud **as you write it** e.g. 'dyke, d ... y ... k ... e'

A **dyke** can be dug by a river to take any water if the river floods.
_____   _____   _____   _____
_____   _____   _____   _____

A **byte** is one unit of computer information.
_____   _____   _____   _____
_____   _____   _____   _____

If there is a lot of **hype** about an event, people build it up a lot.
_____   _____   _____   _____
_____   _____   _____   _____

What **type** of fruit do you like most?
_____   _____   _____   _____
_____   _____   _____   _____

A **tyre** goes around the wheel of a car.
_____   _____   _____   _____
_____   _____   _____   _____

Jazz is one **style** of music.
_____   _____   _____   _____
_____   _____   _____   _____

To **analyse** (a/na/lyse) something means to study it closely.
_____   _____   _____   _____
_____   _____   _____   _____

To **paralyse** (pa/ra/lyse) something means to prevent it moving.
_____   _____   _____   _____
_____   _____   _____   _____

Pirates often have a patch over one **eye**.
_____   _____   _____   _____
_____   _____   _____   _____

Dye is used to add colour to clothes.
_____   _____   _____   _____
_____   _____   _____   _____

Now test yourself without looking at the words and **check for yourself** if you got them all right. Practice writing any words that you made mistakes on again.

The sound (ist) is represented by the letters ist at the end of descriptions of people, like in the words below

Remember: Say the word aloud, then say each letter aloud **as you write it** e.g. 'florist, f ... l ... o ... r ... i ... s ... t'

A **florist (flo/rist)** sells flowers.
_____ _____ _____ _____
_____ _____ _____ _____

An **artist (ar/tist)** creates works of art, like paintings or sculptures.
_____ _____ _____ _____
_____ _____ _____ _____

A **pianist (pi/an/ist)** plays the piano.
_____ _____ _____ _____
_____ _____ _____ _____

A **scientist (sci/en/tist)** studies biology, chemistry or physics.
_____ _____ _____ _____
_____ _____ _____ _____

A **journalist (jour/na/list)** writes or talks about the news.
_____ _____ _____ _____
_____ _____ _____ _____

A **dentist (den/tist)** looks after people's teeth.
_____ _____ _____ _____
_____ _____ _____ _____

A **motorist (mo/to/rist)** drives a vehicle.
_____ _____ _____ _____
_____ _____ _____ _____

A **cyclist (cy/clist)** rides a bike.
_____ _____ _____ _____
_____ _____ _____ _____

A **geologist (ge/ol/o/gist)** studies rocks.
_____ _____ _____ _____
_____ _____ _____ _____

A **chemist (che/mist)** gives people medicine.
_____ _____ _____ _____
_____ _____ _____ _____

Now test yourself without looking at the words and **check for yourself** if you got them all right. Practice writing any words that you made mistakes on again.

The sound (ist) is represented by the letters est at the end of comparing words, like in the words below

Remember: Say the word aloud, then say each letter aloud **as you write it** e.g. 'largest, l ... a ... r ... g ... e ... s ... t'

An elephant is one of the **largest (lar/gest)** animals.
_____ _____ _____   _____
_____ _____ _____   _____

Your **closest (clo/sest)** friends are your best friends.
_____ _____ _____   _____
_____ _____ _____   _____

One plus one is the **simplest (sim/plest)** sum.
_____ _____ _____   _____
_____ _____ _____   _____

Who gets up the **earliest (ear/li/est)** in your house?
_____ _____ _____   _____
_____ _____ _____   _____

One plus one is the **easiest (ea/si/est)** sum.
_____ _____ _____   _____
_____ _____ _____   _____

An elephant is one of the **heaviest (hea/vi/est)** animals.
_____ _____ _____   _____
_____ _____ _____   _____

An elephant is one of the **biggest (big/gest)** animals.
_____ _____ _____   _____
_____ _____ _____   _____

Near the equator is the **hottest (hot/test)** part of the Earth's surface.
_____ _____ _____   _____
_____ _____ _____   _____

Athletes are the **fittest (fit/test)** people around.
_____ _____ _____   _____
_____ _____ _____   _____

The moon is the **nearest (near/est)** thing to the Earth.
_____ _____ _____   _____
_____ _____ _____   _____

Now test yourself without looking at the words and **check for yourself** if you got them all right. Practice writing any words that you made mistakes on again.

The sound (ur) is sometimes represented by the letters our at the end of words, like in the words below

Remember: Say the word aloud, then say each letter aloud **as you write it** e.g. 'armour, a ... r ... m ... o ... u ... r'

Armour (ar/mour) is used to protect a person's body in a fight or a war.
_____ _____ _____ _____
_____ _____ _____ _____

A **harbour (har/bour)** is a place where boats can park.
_____ _____ _____ _____
_____ _____ _____ _____

To do a **favour (fa/vour)** means to do something to help someone out.
_____ _____ _____ _____
_____ _____ _____ _____

What is your favourite **flavour (fla/vour)** of milkshake?
_____ _____ _____ _____
_____ _____ _____ _____

To have a good sense of **humour (hu/mour)** means that you are funny.
_____ _____ _____ _____
_____ _____ _____ _____

An **odour (o/dour)** is a smell.
_____ _____ _____ _____
_____ _____ _____ _____

A **rumour (ru/mour)** is spread between people, but is not always true.
_____ _____ _____ _____
_____ _____ _____ _____

Vapour (va/pour) is another word for gas.
_____ _____ _____ _____
_____ _____ _____ _____

White is the **colour (co/lour)** of your teeth.
_____ _____ _____ _____
_____ _____ _____ _____

Being chosen as a captain of a team is an **honour (ho/nour)**.
_____ _____ _____ _____
_____ _____ _____ _____

Now test yourself without looking at the words and **check for yourself** if you got them all right. Practice writing any words that you made mistakes on again.

The sound (ur) is sometimes represented by the letters or at the end of words, like in the words below

Remember: Say the word aloud, then say each letter aloud **as you write it** e.g. 'ancestor, a ... n ... c ... e ... s ... t ... o ... r'

Your great-granddad is an **ancestor (an/ces/tor)** of yours.
_____ _____ _____ _____
_____ _____ _____ _____

A ship drops an **anchor (an/chor)** so that it will not move.
_____ _____ _____ _____
_____ _____ _____ _____

A **doctor (doc/tor)** works to help people who are sick or injured.
_____ _____ _____ _____

The **equator (e/qua/tor)** is an imaginary line around the middle of the Earth.
_____ _____ _____ _____

You go to **junior (jun/ior)** school before you go to secondary school.
_____ _____ _____ _____

A **senior (sen/ior)** citizen is a person over 65 years of age.
_____ _____ _____ _____

A **major (ma/jor)** problem is a big problem.
_____ _____ _____ _____

A **minor (mi/nor)** problem is a small problem.
_____ _____ _____ _____

You can use a **razor (ra/zor)** to shave with.
_____ _____ _____ _____

A **mayor** is the head person in a town or a city.
_____ _____ _____ _____

Now test yourself without looking at the words and **check for yourself** if you got them all right. Practice writing any words that you made mistakes on again.

The suffix er is sometimes added to a base word to create the name of a job, like in the words below.

Remember: Say the word aloud, then say each letter aloud **as you write it** e.g. 'teacher, t ... e ... a ... c ... h ... e ... r'

A **teacher (teach+er)** works in a school.
_____ _____ _____ _____
_____ _____ _____ _____

The captain of a sports team is the team's **leader (lead+er)**.
_____ _____ _____ _____
_____ _____ _____ _____

Someone who is doing a job is a **worker (work+er)**.
_____ _____ _____ _____
_____ _____ _____ _____

A tennis **player (play+er)** uses a racquet to hit a ball.
_____ _____ _____ _____
_____ _____ _____ _____

A guest **speaker (speak+er)** will often talk about his or her life.
_____ _____ _____ _____
_____ _____ _____ _____

A racing **driver (drive+er)** tries to go quicker than the other drivers.
_____ _____ _____ _____
_____ _____ _____ _____

A **manager (manage+er)** is in charge of other people.
_____ _____ _____ _____
_____ _____ _____ _____

A police **officer (office+er)** tries to catch criminals.
_____ _____ _____ _____
_____ _____ _____ _____

A **skater (skate + er)** can use roller skates or a skateboard.
_____ _____ _____ _____
_____ _____ _____ _____

A **runner (run+er)** needs to be fit so that he or she can run quickly.
_____ _____ _____ _____
_____ _____ _____ _____

Now test yourself without looking at the words and **check for yourself** if you got them all right. Practice writing any words that you made mistakes on again.

The suffix or is sometimes added to a base word to create a description of a person, like in the words below.

Remember: Say the word aloud, then say each letter aloud **as you write it** e.g. 'actor, a ... c ... t ... o ... r'

An **actor (act+or)** performs in plays, TV shows or films.

_____   _____   _____   _____
_____   _____   _____   _____

A film **director (direct+or)** tells the people on set what to do.

_____   _____   _____   _____
_____   _____   _____   _____

A **sailor (sail+or)** is someone who works on a ship.

_____   _____   _____   _____
_____   _____   _____   _____

A **visitor (visit+or)** to your school is someone who is not usually there.

_____   _____   _____   _____
_____   _____   _____   _____

A **professor (profess+or)** works at a university.

_____   _____   _____   _____
_____   _____   _____   _____

A **decorator (decorate+or)** makes a room look better.

_____   _____   _____   _____
_____   _____   _____   _____

A **dictator (dictate+or)** runs a country without being elected.

_____   _____   _____   _____
_____   _____   _____   _____

Someone who is a **survivor (survive+or)** of a plane crash lives through it.

_____   _____   _____   _____
_____   _____   _____   _____

A **narrator (narrate + or)** can be used to tell the story in a play.

_____   _____   _____   _____
_____   _____   _____   _____

A **surveyor (survey+or)** checks that a building is in a good state.

_____   _____   _____   _____
_____   _____   _____   _____

Now test yourself without looking at the words and **check for yourself** if you got them all right. Practice writing any words that you made mistakes on again.

The words below either have the suffix al or the suffix ee added to the end of them.

Remember: Say the word aloud, then say each letter aloud **as you write it** e.g. 'comical, c ... o ... m ... i ... c ... a ... l'

Comical (comic+al) is another word for funny.
_____   _____   _____   _____
_____   _____   _____   _____

In a **musical (music+al)** the actors sing the words.
_____   _____   _____   _____
_____   _____   _____   _____

A **tropical (tropic+al)** area is hot and has a rainy season and a dry season.
_____   _____   _____   _____
_____   _____   _____   _____

A diary is a **personal (person+al)** thing.
_____   _____   _____   _____
_____   _____   _____   _____

You might cry if you feel very **emotional (emotion+al)**.
_____   _____   _____   _____
_____   _____   _____   _____

Each country has a **national (nation+al)** anthem (song).
_____   _____   _____   _____
_____   _____   _____   _____

A **refugee (refuge+ee)** is someone who has been forced to leave his or her home.
_____   _____   _____   _____
_____   _____   _____   _____

A company's **employee (employ+ee)** is someone who works for them.
_____   _____   _____   _____
_____   _____   _____   _____

A **trainee (train+ee)** is someone who is learning to do something.
_____   _____   _____   _____
_____   _____   _____   _____

A prison **escapee (escape+ee)** is someone who has broken out of jail.
_____   _____   _____   _____
_____   _____   _____   _____

Now test yourself without looking at the words and **check for yourself** if you got them all right. Practice writing any words that you made mistakes on again.

The long (e) sound is represented by the letter i in some words, like in the words below.

Remember: Say the word aloud, then say each letter aloud **as you write it** e.g. 'pizza, p ... i ... z ... z ... a'

Pizza (piz/za) has a dough base with tomato puree on it.
_____   _____   _____   _____
_____   _____   _____   _____

A **radiator (ra/di/a/tor)** can be used to heat a room.
_____   _____   _____   _____
_____   _____   _____   _____

India (In/di/a) is a massive country in Asia.
_____   _____   _____   _____
_____   _____   _____   _____

The **police (po/lice)** try to catch criminals.
_____   _____   _____   _____
_____   _____   _____   _____

A **genius (ge/ni/us)** is someone who is extremely intelligent.
_____   _____   _____   _____
_____   _____   _____   _____

A **warrior (war/ri/or)** is another name for a fighter.
_____   _____   _____   _____
_____   _____   _____   _____

An **alien (a/li/en)** is a creature from another planet.
_____   _____   _____   _____
_____   _____   _____   _____

Plastic is one type of **material (ma/te/ri/al)**.
_____   _____   _____   _____
_____   _____   _____   _____

Doing a sky dive is a scary **experience (ex/pe/ri/ence)**.
_____   _____   _____   _____
_____   _____   _____   _____

To use an **alias (a/li/as)** means to use a name that is not really your name.
_____   _____   _____   _____
_____   _____   _____   _____

Now test yourself without looking at the words and **check for yourself** if you got them all right. Practice writing any words that you made mistakes on again.

The long (e) sound is represented by the letter i in some words, like in the words below.

Remember: Say the word aloud, then say each letter aloud **as you write it** e.g. 'piano, p ... i ... a ... n ... o'

A **piano (pi/a/no)** is an instrument with black and white keys to press.
_____ _____ _____ _____
_____ _____ _____ _____

A **patio (pa/ti/o)** is a paved part of a garden for sitting out on.
_____ _____ _____ _____
_____ _____ _____ _____

The **ratio (ra/ti/o)** of children to teachers is 30:1 in most classes.
_____ _____ _____ _____
_____ _____ _____ _____

The **radio (ra/di/o)** has a DJ who plays music.
_____ _____ _____ _____
_____ _____ _____ _____

To be **incognito (in/cog/ni/to)** means to be in disguise.
_____ _____ _____ _____
_____ _____ _____ _____

A **trio (tri/o)** of friends means three friends.
_____ _____ _____ _____
_____ _____ _____ _____

A **champion (cham/pi/on)** is someone who has won something.
_____ _____ _____ _____
_____ _____ _____ _____

If an event goes very badly, it might be described as a **fiasco (fi/a/sco)**.
_____ _____ _____ _____
_____ _____ _____ _____

To **ski** is to put a pair of long, thin boards on your feet and slide on snow.
_____ _____ _____ _____
_____ _____ _____ _____

The **radius (ra/di/us)** of a circle is the distance from its middle to its side.
_____ _____ _____ _____
_____ _____ _____ _____

Now test yourself without looking at the words and **check for yourself** if you got them all right. Practice writing any words that you made mistakes on again.

The sound (j) is sometimes represented by the letter g, like in the words below.

Remember: Say the word aloud, then say each letter aloud **as you write it** e.g. 'legend, l ... e ... g ... e ... n ... d'

A **legend (le/gend)** is an old story that is (at least partly) not true.
_____ _____ _____ _____
_____ _____ _____ _____

An estate **agent (a/gent)** is someone who sells houses.
_____ _____ _____ _____
_____ _____ _____ _____

Geometry (ge/o/me/try) is the study of shapes.
_____ _____ _____ _____
_____ _____ _____ _____

Geography (ge/o/gra/phy) is the study of the Earth's features.
_____ _____ _____ _____
_____ _____ _____ _____

Algebra (al/ge/bra) is a type of maths that uses letters and symbols.
_____ _____ _____ _____
_____ _____ _____ _____

A **stranger (stran/ger)** is someone who you do not know.
_____ _____ _____ _____
_____ _____ _____ _____

A **genre (gen/re)** is a type of writing, such as comedy or science fiction.
_____ _____ _____ _____
_____ _____ _____ _____

In some legends, a **genie (ge/nie)** comes out of a magic lamp.
_____ _____ _____ _____
_____ _____ _____ _____

Hygiene (hy/giene) is about keeping things clean, like washing your hands.
_____ _____ _____ _____
_____ _____ _____ _____

A **genetic (ge/ne/tic)** disease is passed from parents to their children.
_____ _____ _____ _____
_____ _____ _____ _____

Now test yourself without looking at the words and <u>check for yourself</u> if you got them all right. Practice writing any words that you made mistakes on again.

The sound (s) is sometimes represented by the letter c, like in the words below.

Remember: Say the word aloud, then say each letter aloud **as you write it** e.g. 'capacity, c ... a ... p ... a ... c ... i ... t ... y'

The **capacity (ca/pa/city)** of a bottle means how much liquid it can hold.
_____ _____ _____ _____
_____ _____ _____ _____

Temperature can be measured in degrees **centigrade (cen/ti/grade)**.
_____ _____ _____ _____
_____ _____ _____ _____

To give your age in years *and months* is to be **specific (spe/ci/fic)**.
_____ _____ _____ _____
_____ _____ _____ _____

People go to the **cinema (ci/ne/ma)** to watch a film.
_____ _____ _____ _____
_____ _____ _____ _____

A car crash is an example of a serious **incident (in/ci/dent)**.
_____ _____ _____ _____
_____ _____ _____ _____

Falling off a ladder is an example of an **accident (ac/ci/dent)**.
_____ _____ _____ _____
_____ _____ _____ _____

A wedding is an example of a **ceremony (ce/re/mo/ny)**.
_____ _____ _____ _____
_____ _____ _____ _____

People often have a party to **celebrate (ce/le/brate)** their birthday.
_____ _____ _____ _____
_____ _____ _____ _____

Cider (ci/der) is an alcoholic drink that is made from apples.
_____ _____ _____ _____
_____ _____ _____ _____

A **cyclone (cy/clone)** is a very large storm.
_____ _____ _____ _____
_____ _____ _____ _____

Now test yourself without looking at the words and **check for yourself** if you got them all right. Practice writing any words that you made mistakes on again.

The sound (f) is sometimes represented by the letters ph, like in the words below.

Remember: Say the word aloud, then say each letter aloud **as you write it** e.g. 'morph, m ... o ... r ... p ... h'

For something to **morph** means that it quickly changes how it looks.
_____ _____ _____ _____
_____ _____ _____ _____

A **nymph** is a beautiful fairy found near rivers, mountains or woods.
_____ _____ _____ _____
_____ _____ _____ _____

An **aphid (a/phid)** is an insect that feeds by sucking sap from plants.
_____ _____ _____ _____
_____ _____ _____ _____

A **cipher (ci/pher)** is a written code. _____ _____
_____ _____ _____ _____

To **decipher (de/ci/pher)** a code means to work it out
_____ _____ _____ _____
_____ _____ _____ _____

A **hyphen (hy/phen)** is a horizontal punctuation mark (-).
_____ _____ _____ _____
_____ _____ _____ _____

A **pharaoh (pha/raoh)** is an ancient Egyptian king.
_____ _____ _____ _____
_____ _____ _____ _____

To have a **phobia (pho/bi/a)** of spiders means that you are afraid of them.
_____ _____ _____ _____

The first **phase** of school is Early Years.
_____ _____ _____ _____
_____ _____ _____ _____

The English **alphabet (al/pha/bet)** has 26 letters in it.
_____ _____ _____ _____
_____ _____ _____ _____

Now test yourself without looking at the words and **check for yourself** if you got them all right. Practice writing any words that you made mistakes on again.

At the end of a very few words, the sound (un) is represented by the letters eon. The prefix uni means one; for example, a unicorn has one horn.

Remember: Say the word aloud, then say each letter aloud **as you write it** e.g. 'pigeon, p ... i ... g ... e ... o ... n'

A **pigeon (pi/geon)** is a type of bird that is usually grey in towns and cities.
_____ _____ _____ _____
_____ _____ _____ _____

To **bludgeon (blu/dgeon)** something means to hit it very hard.
_____ _____ _____ _____

A **dungeon (dun/geon)** is an underground prison.
_____ _____ _____ _____
_____ _____ _____ _____

A **smidgeon (smi/dgeon)** is a very small amount.
_____ _____ _____ _____
_____ _____ _____ _____

A **surgeon (sur/geon)** performs operations on people.
_____ _____ _____ _____
_____ _____ _____ _____

Do you have to wear a school **uniform (u/ni/form)**?
_____ _____ _____ _____
_____ _____ _____ _____

The right to free speech should be a **universal (u/ni/ver/sal)** human right.
_____ _____ _____ _____
_____ _____ _____ _____

If two groups **unify (u/ni/fy)** that means that they join together.
_____ _____ _____ _____
_____ _____ _____ _____

A choir tries to sing in **unison (u/ni/son)** (at the same time).
_____ _____ _____ _____
_____ _____ _____ _____

A **unicorn (u/ni/corn)** is a mythical creature, like a horse with one horn.
_____ _____ _____ _____
_____ _____ _____ _____

Now test yourself without looking at the words and **check for yourself** if you got them all right. Practice writing any words that you made mistakes on again.

The prefix aer means 'in the air' and the prefix mal means 'not'.

Remember: Say the word aloud, then say each letter aloud **as you write it** e.g. 'aerial, a ...e ... r ... i ... a ... l'

A TV **aerial (ae/ri/al)** receives a TV signal.
_____   _____   _____   _____
_____   _____   _____   _____

To **aerate (ae/rate)** water means to pump air into it.
_____   _____   _____   _____
_____   _____   _____   _____

Aerobic (ae/ro/bic) exercise increases your heart rate.
_____   _____   _____   _____
_____   _____   _____   _____

An **aerosol (ae/ro/sol)** spray is used to make a room or a person smell nice.
_____   _____   _____   _____
_____   _____   _____   _____

An **aeronaut (ae/ro/naut)** is the pilot of an airship or an air balloon.
_____   _____   _____   _____
_____   _____   _____   _____

An **aerodrome (ae/ro/drome)** is a small airport.
_____   _____   _____   _____
_____   _____   _____   _____

An **aeroplane (ae/ro/plane)** flies people or things around.
_____   _____   _____   _____
_____   _____   _____   _____

To suffer from **malnutrition (mal/nu/tri/tion)** is to not have enough to eat.
_____   _____   _____   _____
_____   _____   _____   _____

For a machine to **malfunction (mal/func/tion)** means for it stop working.
_____   _____   _____   _____
_____   _____   _____   _____

A **maladjusted (mal/ad/jus/ted)** person will not get on with other people.
_____   _____   _____   _____
_____   _____   _____   _____

Now test yourself without looking at the words and **check for yourself** if you got them all right. Practice writing any words that you made mistakes on again.

The prefix fore means 'before'. For example, to foresee something is to see it coming before it happens.

Remember: Say the word aloud, then say each letter aloud **as you write it** e.g. 'forecast, f … o … r … e … c … a … s … t'

The weather **forecast (fore/cast)** predicts what the weather will be like.
_____ _____ _____ _____
_____ _____ _____ _____

Your **forehead (fore/head)** is above your eyes.
_____ _____ _____ _____
_____ _____ _____ _____

To **foresee (fore/see)** an event is to see it coming before it happens.
_____ _____ _____ _____

A **foreman (fore/man)** is the man in charge of a group of builders.
_____ _____ _____ _____

The **foreground (fore/ground)** is the part of a picture that appears nearest.
_____ _____ _____ _____

The idea at the **forefront (fore/front)** of your mind is what you are thinking of.
_____ _____ _____ _____

In a book, a **foreword (fore/word)** can come at the start of the book.
_____ _____ _____ _____

A **forecourt (fore/court)** is a space in front of a building that belongs to it.
_____ _____ _____ _____

Your **forefathers (fore/fa/thers)** are the people that came before you.
_____ _____ _____ _____

To **forewarn (fore/warn)** someone is to warn him or her before an event.
_____ _____ _____ _____

Now test yourself without looking at the words and **check for yourself** if you got them all right. Practice writing any words that you made mistakes on again.

Each of the words below begins with a prefix. These are prefixes that are not used in very many words.

Remember: Say the word aloud, then say each letter aloud **as you write it** e.g. 'surreal, s ... u ... r ... r ...e ... a ... l'

If something feels **surreal (sur/real)**, it feels like it is not really happening.

_____ _____ _____ _____
_____ _____ _____ _____

To **surpass (sur/pass)** someone means to overtake him or her.

_____ _____ _____ _____
_____ _____ _____ _____

To **surmount (sur/mount)** an obstacle is to overcome it.

_____ _____ _____ _____
_____ _____ _____ _____

Your **surname (sur/name)** is your last name.

_____ _____ _____ _____
_____ _____ _____ _____

An **intravenous (in/tra/ve/nous)** drip goes straight into your bloodstream.

_____ _____ _____ _____
_____ _____ _____ _____

An **intranet (in/tra/net)** system is only available to members.

_____ _____ _____ _____
_____ _____ _____ _____

To use a **psudonym (pseu/do/nym)** is to use a name that is not your real name.

_____ _____ _____ _____
_____ _____ _____ _____

To be **hypersensitive (hy/per/sen/si/tive)** is to be oversensitive.

_____ _____ _____ _____
_____ _____ _____ _____

A **hyperactive (hy/per/ac/tive)** child finds it hard to sit and concentrate.

_____ _____ _____ _____
_____ _____ _____ _____

Hyperbole (hy/per/bole) is another word for exaggeration.

_____ _____ _____ _____
_____ _____ _____ _____

Now test yourself without looking at the words and **check for yourself** if you got them all right. Practice writing any words that you made mistakes on again.

All of the words below represent a sound in an unusual way. For example, the word ocean uses the letters cean to represent the sound (shun).

Remember: Say the word aloud, then say each letter aloud **as you write it** e.g. 'gross, g ... r ... o ... s ... s'

Gross is another word for disgusting.
_____ _____ _____ _____
_____ _____ _____ _____

A **chimera (chi/me/ra)** is an imaginary animal made up of different animal parts.
_____ _____ _____ _____
_____ _____ _____ _____

An **ocean (o/cean)** is a large sea.
_____ _____ _____ _____
_____ _____ _____ _____

A **recipe (re/ci/pe)** tells you how to cook or to make something to eat.
_____ _____ _____ _____
_____ _____ _____ _____

If you cut yourself, **blood** will come out of the cut.
_____ _____ _____ _____
_____ _____ _____ _____

In a **flood**, water gets into places that it is not supposed to.
_____ _____ _____ _____
_____ _____ _____ _____

A person's **figure (fi/gure)** is the shape of his or her body.
_____ _____ _____ _____
_____ _____ _____ _____

A **choir** is a group of people singing together.
_____ _____ _____ _____
_____ _____ _____ _____

Papaya (pa/pa/ya) is a sphere-shaped fruit with yellow pulp.
_____ _____ _____ _____
_____ _____ _____ _____

The **area (a/re/a)** of a shpa is the amount of space inside it.
_____ _____ _____ _____
_____ _____ _____ _____

Now test yourself without looking at the words and **check for yourself** if you got them all right. Practice writing any words that you made mistakes on again.

All of the words below represent a sound in an unusual way. For example, the word sieve has a silent e in the middle of it.

Remember: Say the word aloud, then say each letter aloud **as you write it** e.g. 'sieve, s ... i ... e ... v ... e'

A **sieve** is used for removing bits from liquids, like orange juice.
_____ _____ _____ _____
_____ _____ _____ _____

A **penguin (pen/guin)** is a bird that can swim, but is not able to fly.
_____ _____ _____ _____
_____ _____ _____ _____

A **quay** is a platform where people can get on and off boats.
_____ _____ _____ _____
_____ _____ _____ _____

A **cupboard (cup/board)** is used for storing things.
_____ _____ _____ _____
_____ _____ _____ _____

A **draught** is an unwanted breeze that comes into a place through a gap.
_____ _____ _____ _____
_____ _____ _____ _____

A **sovereign (so/ve/reign)** is a king or a queen.
_____ _____ _____ _____
_____ _____ _____ _____

Biscuit (bis/cuit) is a dry, crumbly type of food.
_____ _____ _____ _____
_____ _____ _____ _____

Suede is a material like leather with a velvety surface.
_____ _____ _____ _____
_____ _____ _____ _____

Foliage (fo/li/age) is another name for the leaves of a plant or a tree.
_____ _____ _____ _____
_____ _____ _____ _____

To be in **awe** of someone is to be amazed by that person.
_____ _____ _____ _____
_____ _____ _____ _____

Now test yourself without looking at the words and <u>check for yourself</u> if you got them all right. Practice writing any words that you made mistakes on again.

All of the words below represent a sound in an unusual way. For example, the word brooch uses the letters oo to represent the long (o) sound.

Remember: Say the word aloud, then say each letter aloud **as you write it** e.g. 'abyss, a ... b ... y ... s ... s'

An **abyss (a/byss)** is a massive hole.

_____ _____ _____ _____

_____ _____ _____ _____

A **brooch** is a piece of jewellery that it pinned on to your clothes.

_____ _____ _____ _____

_____ _____ _____ _____

People race around a **circuit (cir/cuit)**.

_____ _____ _____ _____

_____ _____ _____ _____

A **cello (cel/lo)** is a large string instrument.

_____ _____ _____ _____

_____ _____ _____ _____

Climate (cli/mate) is average weather over a long period of time.

_____ _____ _____ _____

_____ _____ _____ _____

A **tsunami (tsu/na/mi)** is a giant wave caused by an underwater earthquake.

_____ _____ _____ _____

_____ _____ _____ _____

Larvae (lar/vae) grow into insects.

_____ _____ _____ _____

_____ _____ _____ _____

A **coyote (co/yo/te)** is a type of wild dog.

_____ _____ _____ _____

_____ _____ _____ _____

Colonel is a rank in the army.

_____ _____ _____ _____

_____ _____ _____ _____

Some eskimos live in an **igloo (ig/loo)**.

_____ _____ _____ _____

_____ _____ _____ _____

Now test yourself without looking at the words and **check for yourself** if you got them all right. Practice writing any words that you made mistakes on again.

All of the words below end in the letters gue, the letters que or the letters quet.

Remember: Say the word aloud, then say each letter aloud **as you write it** e.g. 'racquet, r ... a ... c ... q ... u ... e ... t'

A tennis player uses a **racquet (rac/quet)** to hit the ball.

_____   _____   _____   _____
_____   _____   _____   _____

In **croquet (cro/quet)** you use a hammer to hit a ball through a gate.

_____   _____   _____   _____
_____   _____   _____   _____

A **bouquet (bou/quet)** is made up of flowers arranged to look attractive.

_____   _____   _____   _____
_____   _____   _____   _____

A **banquet (ban/quet)** is a large meal for a lot of people.

_____   _____   _____   _____
_____   _____   _____   _____

Picturesque (pic/tu/resque) is another word for beautiful.

_____   _____   _____   _____
_____   _____   _____   _____

Grotesque (gro/tesque) means very ugly.

_____   _____   _____   _____
_____   _____   _____   _____

A **plague** is a disease that spreads quickly and kills a lot of people.

_____   _____   _____   _____
_____   _____   _____   _____

A person's **physique (phy/sique)** is the size and shape of his or her body.

_____   _____   _____   _____
_____   _____   _____   _____

A **boutique (bou/tique)** is a small clothes shop.

_____   _____   _____   _____
_____   _____   _____   _____

If you feel **fatigue (fa/tigue)**, you feel tired.

_____   _____   _____   _____
_____   _____   _____   _____

Now test yourself without looking at the words and **check for yourself** if you got them all right. Practice writing any words that you made mistakes on again.

The long (o) sound is sometimes represented by the letter o on its own at the end of words, like in the words below.

Remember: Say the word aloud, then say each letter aloud **as you write it** e.g. 'dojo, d … o … j … o'

A **dojo (do/jo)** is a place where people train for judo.

_____ _____ _____ _____
_____ _____ _____ _____

To **veto (ve/to)** an idea or a suggested law means to block it.

_____ _____ _____ _____

A **memo (me/mo)** is a short written message.

_____ _____ _____ _____
_____ _____ _____ _____

A **euro (eu/ro)** is a coin that is used in Europe.

_____ _____ _____ _____

Polo (po/lo) is a game played by riding horses and hitting a ball.

_____ _____ _____ _____

A **cameo (ca/me/o)** is a short performance in a film, play or TV show.

_____ _____ _____ _____

The **tempo (tem/po)** of music is about the speed of the music.

_____ _____ _____ _____
_____ _____ _____ _____

Jumbo (jum/bo) means very big.

_____ _____ _____ _____

Children can visit Santa in his **grotto (grot/to)** at Christmas time.

_____ _____ _____ _____
_____ _____ _____ _____

Tobacco (to/bac/co) is a plant that is used to make cigarettes.

_____ _____ _____ _____
_____ _____ _____ _____

Now test yourself without looking at the words and <u>**check for yourself**</u> if you got them all right. Practice writing any words that you made mistakes on again.

Passwords for Year 6 Spelling Games on www.SaveTeachersSundays.com

Password	Spelling games
ver4x	-cious games
x56bi	-tious games
cw23z	-cial games
byi89	-tial games
ol30c	-ant games
vj30l	-ent 1 games
ni20x	-ent 2 games
bop23	-ent 3 games
w2zer	-ance games
r45vo	-ence games
t6nuo	-ancy and -ency games
t9iop	-able games
iu4fp	-ible games
fkn30	Suffix able (just add)
skn5t	Suffix able (change y to i or drop the e)
dki3o	Suffix able (keep the e)
l2zo8	i before e, except after c 1 games
keol5	i before e, except after c 2 games
cwz2f	-ough games
fr7ki	-ought and -aught games
cqz23	gu- games
vk50m	-mb games
dlo4n	Silent l and -mn games
ghio5	rh-, gh- and -bt games
vleo4	Other silent letters games
xse34	Homophones and Confusable Words 1 games

Passwords for Year 6 Spelling Games on www.SaveTeachersSundays.com

Password	Spelling games
f46bj	Homophones and Confusable Words 2 games
mdi80	Homophones and Confusable Words 3 games
ce34b	Hyphenated prefixes games
nlop5	Prefix fore games
hpo4n	Prefix aer and prefix mal games
zpl34	Prefix uni and -eon (e.g. surgeon) games
vl34d	Other Prefixes games
ve34x	Adding Suffixes to -fer words games
vwz3c	Suffix er games
ct67u	Suffix or games
br5ct	Suffix est games
iolp0	Suffix ist games
nr67b	Suffix al and suffix ee games
cqz8l	Year 5 and 6 word list 1 words games
l3d8k	Year 5 and 6 word list 2 words games
j7k9o	Year 5 and 6 word list 3 words games
pd3f6	Year 5 and 6 word list 4 words games
vex4h	Year 5 and 6 word list 5 words games
hi40v	Year 5 and 6 word list 6 words games
bfq2p	Year 5 and 6 word list 7 words games
pzk3l	Year 5 and 6 word list 8 words games
vmt5o	-ar(e.g. calendar) games
cl3lx	-er (e.g. member) games
cl2a0	-ard (e.g. forward) games
o3k3l	-ary (e.g. library) games
vex34	-ine (in) games

Passwords for Year 6 Spelling Games on www.SaveTeachersSundays.com

Password	Spelling games
m78ki	-ine (een) games
ko90l	-ice games
cw23z	-ite and -it games
ny78k	-ate games
bo4px	-our games
xp4lb	-or games
nt7io	-ous games
ne3co	-us games
ve3z0	Soft c 2 games
br56n	Soft g 2 games
be3x4	-tion games
muo9l	-ation games
m30cn	-sion games
jr4v8	-ssion games
kia0l	-cian and -ture games
vex0m	(f) as ph 2 games
ve4by	-gue, -que and -quet games
cex0o	Irregular Words 1 games
bk50l	Irregular Words 2 games
vn2ia	Irregular Words 3 games
cwz3b	Long (e) as i 1 games
nt8lp	Long (e) as i 2 games
ve5bi	Long (o) as o at the end of words 2 games
im3vo	Long (u) as eu and (sh) as ch games
cwz0m	ou games
nol4p	y-e words games

9561138R00048

Printed in Great Britain
by Amazon.co.uk, Ltd.,
Marston Gate.